S0-DPQ-351

Library of
Davidson College

# INTERPRETATIONS
# OF PLATO

*A Swarthmore Symposium*

# MNEMOSYNE

## BIBLIOTHECA CLASSICA BATAVA

COLLEGERUNT

W. DEN BOER · W. J. VERDENIUS · R. E. H. WESTENDORP BOERMA

BIBLIOTHECAE FASCICULOS EDENDOS CURAVIT

W. J. VERDENIUS, HOMERUSLAAN 53, ZEIST

SUPPLEMENTUM QUINQUAGESIMUM

HELEN F. NORTH (ED.)

## INTERPRETATIONS OF PLATO

*A Swarthmore Symposium*

LUGDUNI BATAVORUM E. J. BRILL MCMLXXVII

# INTERPRETATIONS OF PLATO

*A Swarthmore Symposium*

EDITED BY

HELEN F. NORTH

LUGDUNI BATAVORUM E. J. BRILL MCMLXXVII

184
P71xn

81-6241

ISBN    90 04 05262 3

Copyright 1977 by E. J. Brill, Leiden, The Netherlands

All rights reserved. No part of this book may be reproduced or
translated in any form, by print, photoprint, microfilm, microfiche
or any other means without written permission from the publisher

PRINTED IN THE NETHERLANDS

# TABLE OF CONTENTS

# PREFACE

According to Porphyry Plotinus used to offer sacrifice and entertain his friends on the traditional birthdays of Plato and Socrates. At these celebrations, such of his friends as were capable (*dunatoi*) were expected to read a discourse before the assembled company. On one occasion Porphyry himself read a poem on the Sacred Marriage, expressed in such mysterious and veiled language that someone in the audience said he was mad. The rhetor Diophanes read a defence of Alcibiades in Plato's *Symposium* which so upset Plotinus that he encouraged Porphyry to compose a refutation.

In 1974 the classical world celebrated what was reckoned to be the two thousand-four-hundredth birthday of Plato. When Swarthmore College, with the support of the William J. Cooper Foundation, undertook to share in the festivities, it seemed appropriate to invite four distinguished Platonists, incontestably *dunatoi*, to read papers in his honor. Since it would have been impossible to do justice to the whole of Plato's philosophy in one weekend in November, we simply asked our lecturers to share with us the fruits of their current research. No effort was made to concentrate on any particular area of Platonic studies or to co-ordinate the topics in any way. The unity that we sought was to proceed solely from the One that was Plato—to speak in a Plotinian way—and emanate to the Many that were in the audience.

The result was a series, Platonic to be sure in its unity, but also in its diversity, and for that reason all the more satisfactory as a celebration of more than two millennia of Plato's influence. Not only do these four lectures confront different aspects of Plato's influence; they represent a variety of approaches. Two of them adopt a chronological point of view; two put their emphasis on special subjects or methods of philosophizing, without regard for chronological development. The lecture-form has been preserved. Modest additions and revisions have been made, and the lecturers have been given the opportunity to supply Notes. All four lectures, in different ways, expand our vision beyond Plato himself and demonstrate the richness and diversity of his impact on later thought. The festivities were such, we think, as Plotinus would have approved.

HELEN F. NORTH
Swarthmore College

# THE THEORY OF SOCIAL JUSTICE IN THE *POLIS* IN PLATO'S *REPUBLIC* [1]

## GREGORY VLASTOS

A few years ago an international committee of classical scholars decided that 1974 was to be the 2,400th anniversary of Plato's birth. The computations which led them to this result are no concern of mine: I have no desire to look this gift horse in the mouth. I accept it "without prejudice," as the lawyers say, welcoming it as a ceremonial date which offers a once-in-a-lifetime challenge to take stock of Plato's achievement in its entirety and reassess each of his many-sided contributions to Western thought. With this in view I put this question to myself. "What is that aspect of Plato's thought which has suffered the most in my lifetime through misunderstanding or neglect?" To this my answer has been, unhesitatingly, "his theory of social justice." If other students of Plato disagree, as they well may, I shall not anticipate their objections and try to bring them around to my view: this would require a critical review of what has been written on this topic in the last half-century—an undertaking which would call for a major monograph all by itself. All I can do here is to remind them that once the storm unleashed by the chapter on this topic in Sir Karl Popper's *The Open Society and its Enemies* had blown

[1] This paper was to have been my contribution to a symposium celebrating the 2,400th anniversary of Plato's birth at an international congress of classical scholars in Madrid in August, 1974. When I withdrew (for political reasons) from that congress, I was able to avail myself of another chance to participate at an academic celebration of that anniversary at Swarthmore College in November, 1974. The first draft of this paper was written for the latter occasion. It has been subsequently revised and much documentation has been added—in fact, considerably more than could be accommodated within the present volume. A more complete version of this paper will appear in a book I expect to publish shortly, dealing with various aspects of Plato's theory of social justice. I wish to express thanks for criticisms or suggestions from various scholars who have read or heard earlier drafts, including Professors R. E. Allen, Harold Cherniss, Daniel Devereux, Andreas Graeser, G. F. Hourani, David Gauthier, Warner Morse, Martin Ostwald, Michael Rohr, Christopher Rowe, Laszlo Versenyi, and A. D. Woozley.

over—a decade after the publication of his book (1945) [2]—no study in depth of Plato's theory of social justice has appeared in English,[3] though in the past two decades journal articles and books on Plato have been pouring out in greater volume than ever before. So there should be room for a new assessment of what is after all by common consent the first full-blown philosophical theory of justice in the western world.

Since the space at my disposal is limited, the theory I shall discuss here is exclusively the one in the *Republic*.[4] This is where Plato expounds first and in the fullest terms his novel conception of social justice. On that topic he has virtually nothing further to say until he comes to write the *Laws*. To that last work of his we have to look for his second thoughts on social justice. But these would have no great interest for us if we had not known those first ones which he now tacitly amends. Of this fearless self-correction I shall have a word to say at the end. For the rest I shall

---

[2] See Appendix A. My references to the book (all of them by author's name only) will be to the reprint of the (revised and enlarged) fourth edition in the Harper Torchbook series (New York, 1962).

[3] In marked contrast to the plethora of work on and around what Plato calls "the justice of a private man," much of it triggered by a paper by David Sachs, "A Fallacy in Plato's *Republic*," *Philosophical Review* 73 (1964), 141-159: this essay was followed by series of papers during the next decade, all of them concerned primarily (some of them exclusively) with psychic, in contrast to political, justice. The thinness of the literature on Plato's theory of social justice in the 'fifties and 'sixties may be verified by a glance at the bibliographical listings in the section on the *Republic* in H. Cherniss, *Lustrum* 4 (1960), 153 ff. (more titles, but not much more substance, in the section on "Politics and Society" in the sequel, *Lustrum* 5 (1960), 470 ff.). The 'sixties marked the appearance of R. C. Cross and A.D. Woozley, *Plato's Republic: a Philosophical Commentary* (1964); Donald Kagan, *The Great Debate: History of Political Thought From Homer to Polybius* (1965); and Sheldon Wolin, *Politics and Vision* (1960, 28-68): there are noteworthy remarks on Plato's theory of social justice in each of these, but none of the three deal with the topic in sufficient depth and detail.

[4] And in the *Republic* itself I shall discuss only the norm encapsulated in the "doing one's own" definiens (433A-B), which involves the just relations of persons and classes *within* the πόλις and *to* the πόλις: the quoted catch-phrase is introduced (433A8) as a contraction for a fuller definiens (433A4-6) where what comes to be called "one's own" in the catch-phrase is clearly and unambiguously a function "which concerns the πόλις" (ἕν . . . τῶν περὶ τὴν πόλιν). Let me emphasize that this norm is not meant to determine

(a) what a πόλις owes to other πόλεις, or
(b) what individual members of a πόλις owe to individual members of other πόλεις, or
(c) what persons who are not members of a πόλις owe to anyone else.

be glad to keep within the covers of the composition which is by general consent the greatest product of his genius.[5]

## I

But first I must try to establish that there is such a thing as a theory of *justice* in that dialogue whose formal theme is δικαιοσύνη. As is well known,[6] this word is no true equivalent of our "justice." Why should we then assume that what ours denotes is what Plato's theory is all about?[7] To this day the question has gone unanswered. It has yet to be made clear why it is that when we impute to Plato a theory of justice in the *Republic* on the strength of what he says there about δικαιοσύνη we are not being the victims of a fossilized mistranslation. Let me then try to prove what heretofore has been so frequently assumed without proof. To this purely semantic argument I shall devote the first few pages of this paper.

Aristotle, with his good ear for ambiguity, is the first to notice the one in δικαιοσύνη. He resolves it in the opening paragraphs of Book V of the *Nicomachean Ethics*.[8] Δικαιοσύνη is used, he says, both as a generic term—for "complete" (i.e. comprehensive) social virtue [9]—yet also as the name of *a* social virtue—for "a

---

[5] It should go without saying that, even so, all I shall attempt to offer will be the elements of the theory—its bare essentials. What I present here may be supplemented to some small extent by earlier remarks on Plato's social and political theory in my *Platonic Studies* (Princeton, 1973) in the following passages: 11-19, 32, 117-126; 146-53; 192-203; 210-17. (To this work I shall refer hereafter by the abbreviation "*PS*.")

[6] Though seldom expressly recognized. Even Paul Shorey, usually so sensitive to the value of Greek words, does not discuss the problem either in his translation (listed in the bibliographical "Additional Note" at the conclusion of the notes, below) or in his analysis of the *Republic* in *What Plato Said* (Chicago, 1933), 208 ff. But there are honourable exceptions. Thus R. C. Cross and A. D. Woozley (*Plato's "Republic," a Philosophical Commentary* [London, 1964; hereafter I shall refer to this book by its authors' names only]) say in their Preface that " 'justice' is a thoroughly unsuitable word to use as a translation of the Greek word"; they resign themselves to it because "there is now so little hope of changing the usage."

[7] *Pace* demurrers, scholars who have been writing on the *Republic* give every impression of making this assumption. In my essay "The Argument in the *Republic* that 'Justice Pays,' *Journal of Philosophy* 65 (1968), 665-754 (reprinted in corrected and expanded form in *PS*, 111 ff.) I sidestepped the problem, saying I would use *justice* and *just* "merely as counters."

[8] Having adverted to the ambiguity earlier in the *N.E.* (1108B7-8, περὶ δὲ δικαιοσύνης, ἐπεὶ οὐχ ἁπλῶς λέγεται . . .) and still earlier, in the *Topics* (106B29, εἰ γὰρ τὸ δικαίως πολλαχῶς λέγεται . . .).

[9] ἀρετή . . . τελεία, ἀλλ' οὐχ ἁπλῶς ἀλλὰ πρὸς ἕτερον, 1129B26-27; οὐ μέρος ἀρετῆς, ἀλλ' ὅλη ἀρετή, 1130A9. The second of these two descriptions is the

particular δικαιοσύνη" (ἐν μέρει, or κατὰ μέρος, δικαιοσύνη, 1130B
16-17 and 30),[10] whose semantic identity he pins down in two
ways: first, by associating it with "equality," [11] defining it as
"proportional" [12] or "geometrical" [13] equality; secondly, by con-
trasting it with πλεονεξία.[14] In the *Rhetoric* he takes a different
tack. To the ambiguity in δικαιοσύνη he does not here allude at all.
And the terms he now uses to define the word are quite different:
"the virtue because of which each has his own (τὰ αὑτῶν ... ἔχουσιν)
and in conformity with the law." He follows this up with a matching
definiens of ἀδικία as "(the vice) because of which each has what is
another's (τὰ ἀλλότρια [ἔχουσιν]) and not in conformity with the
law" (1366B9-11). Which sense of δικαιοσύνη and its antonym is
being defined here? The wider or the narrower one?

Consider the phrases τὰ αὑτοῦ ἔχειν, τὰ ἀλλότρια ἔχειν. By suitable
use of possessive or reflexive pronouns the Greeks could refer to
property-rights. By means of them they could make the fundamental juristic distinction for which they, unlike the Romans, had no
special terms: [15] the one between possession and ownership—
between the *fact* of having something in one's own use and control
and the *right* to so use and control it. By the use of these phrases
that distinction could be made not only in the domain of property-
rights, but far beyond it. Consider the following from Demosthenes:[16] Having remarked that Philip would be stupid if he thought
the Athenians had meant to cede to him Amphipolis just because

---

one to which he alludes most frequently in the sequel (1130A23, B7, 12, 18,
19, 25): it is the all-inclusiveness of δικαιοσύνη as social virtue (and of ἀδικία
as social vice) that distinguishes this first use of the word; so τελεία in the
first description must have the sense of "complete" rather than "perfect."

[10] A "part" of (social) virtue (μέρος ἀρετῆς, 1130A9).

[11] τὸ ἴσον, 1129A34 and 1130B9; τὸ δίκαιον ἴσον, ὅπερ καὶ ἄνευ λόγου δοκεῖ
πᾶσιν, 1131A13-14. Cf. n. 62 to p. 19 below.

[12] τὸ μὲν οὖν δίκαιον τοῦτο, τὸ ἀνάλογον, 1131B16, the latter being a contraction (cf. τοῦ ἴσου τοῦ κατ' ἀναλογίαν, 1134A5-6).

[13] καλοῦσι δὲ τὴν τοιαύτην ἀναλογίαν γεωμετρικὴν οἱ μαθηματικοί, 1131B12-13.

[14] This contrast is his major clue to the discrimination of the narrower
use of δικαιοσύνη from the wider one: he does the job by picking out the
narrower use of ἀδικία which is covered by πλεονεξία (1130A17 ff.: cf. *PS*,
116).

[15] Classical Greek contains no technical counterparts to the terms by
which this distinction (between *possessio* [from *possedere*, literally "to sit
upon"], on one hand, and *dominium* or *proprietas*, on the other) is upheld in
Roman law. κτάομαι can be used to mean either to *possess* or to *own* (examples
of both uses in *LSJ*).

[16] 7 (*On Halonnesus*), 26.

they had passed a decree that he was to "have" (i.e. keep) what he "had" (i.e. held),[17] Demosthenes proceeds:

> For it is also possible to have what is another's (ἔστι γὰρ ἔχειν τἀλλότρια)— not all who have something have what is their own (οὐχ ἅπαντες οἱ ἔχοντες τὰ αὐτῶν ἔχουσι).[18]

Since what is under dispute is not Philip's ownership of some real estate, but his sovereignty over a Greek city, it is clear that Demosthenes is taking the phrases τὰ αὐτοῦ/τὰ ἀλλότρια ἔχειν as unrestricted to property-rights, hence easily applicable in this case to political rights as well. This leaves no reasonable doubt that when those same phrases turn up in Aristotle's definitions of δικαιοσύνη and ἀδικία in the *Rhetoric*, in a context where they are perfectly general, totally unattached to any specific right of any sort, their reference must be so inclusive as to cover all possible rights;[19] so "the virtue because of which each has his own" must be the one which secures to each of those affected by its exercise the unimpaired possession and enjoyment of their rights. This being the case, there could be no doubt as to which of those two senses of δικαιοσύνη which had been sorted out in the *Ethics* Aristotle is now defining in the *Rhetoric*: When the definiens refers to a virtue whose exercise has that result, what else but "justice" could the definiendum be? I for one, know of no better way of defining "justice" than as the

---

17 ἔχειν αὐτὸν ἃ εἶχεν. The intent of the decree was that existing sovereignties should be preserved (Philip was to *own* what he had previously *owned*), hence that the Athenian title to Amphipolis ("recognized by all Greeks and by the King of Persia," *ibid.*, 29) should remain inviolate. Philip's "stupid sophism" (τὸ σοφὸν αὐτοῦ ἠλίθιον, *loc. cit.*) gave normative force to the first occurrence, factual to the second: he is to *own* what he now *holds* (having annexed it by force).

18 I.e. not all who possess something have a good title to its ownership.

19 The parallel use of *suum* in Roman jurisprudence is instructive. Comparing the two definitions of *iustitia* quoted from Ulpian at the start of the *Digest of the Institutes of Justinian* (both of them take-offs from a Greek original, the definiens of δικαιοσύνη which Plato ascribes to Simonides of Ceos in *Rep.* I, 332A, τὰ ὀφειλόμενα ἑκάστῳ ἀποδιδόναι),

(1) *iustitia* (*est*) *suum cuique tribuere*,

(2) *iustitia est constans et perpetua voluntas ius suum cuique tribuere*,

we can see that Ulpian, whose native tongue, unlike Aristotle's, does furnish him with *ius* a special term for our "right" (the sense in which we speak of "a right to . . ." is conserved perfectly in expressions like *ius testandi, ius connubii,* and so forth), feels free to use *suum* in (1) as a mere contraction for what is expressed more fully by *ius suum* in (2), thus relying on "one's own" to have fully as general and abstract a signification as "one's own right."

disposition to govern one's conduct by respect for the rights of those whom that conduct affects.[20]

Let us then come to Plato with those two uses of δικαιοσύνη tracked down by Aristotle: first as a generic term for which the biblical word "righteousness" would be our nearest equivalent, and then as a species of that genus which we know to be the very one we call "justice."[21] Was Plato using δικαιοσύνη in the first of these two senses, or in the second, or in some third sense, when he defined it in Book IV (433A-B) as "doing one's own," using here this popular catch-phrase for the first time [22] as philosopher's short-hand for the much longer expression which precedes it in the text:

> each single person's pursuing that single practice in [23] the πόλις which his own nature is best fitted to pursue (433A5-6).[24]

---

[20] I have encountered nothing better since submitting many years ago (in "Justice and Equality" in *Social Justice*, ed. by R. Brandt [Englewood Cliffs, N. J., 1962], 53) the following definition:
An action is *just* if, and only if, it is prescribed exclusively by regard for the rights of all whom it affects substantially.
(Hereafter I shall refer to this essay by title only).

[21] The dictionaries blur this vital distinction by allowing "righteous" or "upright" as a normal use of "just," along with that of "equitable" or "impartial" (so *The Shorter Oxford English Dictionary* and *Webster's New Collegiate Dictionary*), ignoring the fact that this would be true enough of earlier usage (e.g. in the King James' Version of the Bible) but that the use of "just" to mean "righteous" is now so rare as to be virtually an archaism. For sensitive comment on the idiomatic use of "justice" see H. L. A. Hart, *The Concept of Law* (Oxford, 1961), 153 ff.

[22] Plato had not so used it in any earlier passage—not even in the *Republic*. The same words occur in 370A4 (ἀλλ' αὐτὸν δι' αὐτὸν τὰ αὐτοῦ πράττει) but there they carry only the ordinary, commonplace, sense of "doing one's own work," and the clause I have cited is being used to designate the *un*specialized, Jack-of-all-trades, activity (the very opposite of Platonic δικαιοσύνη!) to which one would be forced if one lacked the privilege of living in a functionally articulated economic society which allows each person to specialize in the one kind of work he can do best, *this* being the primitive "adumbration" of δικαιοσύνη (ἀρχήν τε καὶ τύπον τινα τῆς δικαιοσύνης, 443C1-2) at the lowest, purely economic, form of human association.

[23] I settle reluctantly for this weakening of the force of the preposition in τῶν περὶ τὴν πόλιν (with precedents in Lindsay, Shorey, Cornford), having failed to hit on a closer rendering without indulging in such over-translation as Robin's, "parmi les fonctions qui intéressent l'État." (For a listing of the translations to which I refer here and elsewhere in this paper see the "additional note" at the end.)

[24] Cf. the fuller expansion of the "doing one's own" phrase I gave in *PS* (119) with its supporting texts:
engaging in that form of social conduct which constitutes the greatest possible contribution which nature has fitted one to make to the happiness and excellence of one's πόλις.

If this is the definiens, what is the definiendum being used to mean—"righteousness", or "justice", or something else?

That it is not "righteousness" I take to be a sure inference from the first of the three arguments by which Plato supports his definition: the non-identity of δικαιοσύνη with wisdom or with courage or with σωφροσύνη—all three of them treated in this context as forms of social, no less than personal, excellence [25]—is a premise of that argument. Plato argues (433B7-E1; and cf. also 427E-428A) that what is denoted by "doing one's own" is of such vast importance for the excellence of a πόλις that it must have one of the great generally recognized social virtues as its name, and that this name can only be δικαιοσύνη, for each of the others has been otherwise accounted for. The validity of this inference has been often attacked and the truth of its premises has been denied, particularly with respect to the alleged non-identity of δικαιοσύνη with σωφροσύνη which, it has been claimed, are as good as synonyms in Plato's idiolect.[26] I would defend Plato on this last count,[27] though not on the first.[28] But neither attack nor defense would be

---

[25] Plato could hardly have been more emphatic on this point: he defines each of them first as a social virtue in the πόλις (427E-432A) and then, much later (442B11-D1), as a personal virtue (an excellence of soul).

[26] C. W. Larson, "The Platonic Synonyms, δικαιοσύνη and σωφροσύνη," *American Journal of Philology* 72 (1951), 395-414.

[27] The criticism is misconceived in so far as it rests on the assumption that if Plato thinks of those two names as necessarily co-extensive (as he, of course, does) he *must* be using them as synonyms. Cf. "equilateral triangle" and "equiangular triangle": the phrases are necessarily co-extensive, but who would wish to say that they are synonymous? Cf. *PS*, 232, n. 27 *sub fin.*

[28] Plato would be justified in assuming, as he does in this argument, that

  (a) the word δικαιοσύνη names a social virtue whose importance to the (moral) excellence of a πόλις is second to none, and

  (b) this virtue is not identical with any of the three he has so far identified.

If he had then drawn his conclusion by merely *assuming* that

  (c) this virtue is identical with the one denoted by his proposed definiens for δικαιοσύνη,

he would have been guilty of an obvious *petitio principii*. But the fact is that he *argues* for (c); it must be true, he claims, because

  (d) the virtue denoted by his proposed definiens is the one which makes it possible for a πόλις to come to have, and to retain, each of those other three virtues.

If (d) were true, it would be a very respectable reason for the truth of (c). Plato assumes that (d) is intuitively true: his Socrates need only state it in that rotund nine-line period (433C4-D5) to elicit Glaucon's unhesitating concurrence. Unhappily, it will not strike others in the same way. Perhaps Plato thinks it will by the time they have read the rest of the *Republic* and have had the chance to see for themselves how much can be expected from

even remotely relevant to the only point I need to make here, namely that Plato is at least as sure of the non-identity of δικαιοσύνη with each of his other great social virtues as of the correctness of his proposed definiens. If he were not, he would not have given us this argument.

May we then without further ado proceed by simple elimination, to infer that since he is not using δικαιοσύνη to mean "righteousness" in this passage, he must be using it to mean "justice"? That would be too easy. For it is no secret that Plato's use of language can be boldly—even perplexingly—revisionary.[29] So how can we be sure that his redefinition of δικαιοσύνη is not being offered in that vein? Clearly we can not without further evidence. Do we have such evidence? I want to argue that we do.

First of all, we can assure ourselves that when at the start of Book II Glaucon poses the great question, "Is δικαιοσύνη profitable?" he is using the word to mean not "righteousness" in general, but "justice" in particular. Of this we have two-fold evidence:

(a) His language anticipates both of the devices Aristotle is to use in the *Nicomachean Ethics* to isolate the narrow use of δικαιοσύνη from the generic one: Glaucon pairs no less closely δικαιοσύνη with equality and ἀδικία with πλεονεξία; he uses "respect for equality" (τὴν τοῦ ἴσου τιμήν) as a simple variant for "respect for justice" (359C6), and πλεονεξία as equivalent to ἀδικία (359C5).

(b) Glaucon's conception of δικαιοσύνη and ἀδικία conforms perfectly to the Aristotelian definitions of these terms in the *Rhetoric*; he uses "to abstain from what is another's" (ἀπέχεσθαι τῶν ἀλλοτρίων, 360B6) and "to keep hands off what is another's" (μὴ ἅπτεσθαι [τῶν ἀλλοτρίων], 360B6; and cf. 360D4) as equivalents of ἀδικεῖν.

Secondly, we can assure ourselves that this use of δικαιοσύνη, so prominent in Glaucon's speech in Book II, has not faded out by the time Plato has reached the "doing one's own" definiens in Book IV. The evidence for this comes in the second of the three

---

the instantiation of "doing one's own" in his ideal πόλις. In that case he is forecasting our eventual agreement; but a forecast is not an argument, so the *petitio* is still being incurred.

[29] Cf. my remarks in *PS*, 115-17 on the extraordinary redefinition of "individual" δικαιοσύνη as "psychic harmony" in 443C9 ff.

arguments (433E3-434A1) in support of that definiens: Holding that

    (1) judges (in the ideal πόλις) [30] instantiate δικαιοσύνη

*because*

    (2) it is their aim [31] to insure that neither litigant "shall have what is another's or be deprived of his own" (μήτ' ἔχωσι τἀλλότρια μήτε τῶν αὑτῶν στέρωνται),

it follows, Plato claims, that

    (3) "the doing and the having of what is one's own (ἡ τοῦ ... ἑαυτοῦ ἕξις τε καὶ πρᾶξις)" is δικαιοσύνη.[32]

This claim enables us to see how "doing one's own" ties up with "having one's own" in Plato's thinking: He is assuming [33] that where $A$ is "doing his own" with reference to $B$ and $C$, $A$ is acting with the intention that $B$ shall have $B$'s own and $C$ shall have $C$'s own and neither of them shall have what is another's, and that it is because $A$'s action is governed by this intention that his conduct towards $B$ and $C$ instantiates δικαιοσύνη. And Plato is counting on this hook-up between the "doing one's own" by $A$ and the "having

---

[30] That this is what is meant is clear from the imperative (προστάξεις δικάσειν): "you" (i.e. the legislation we are now proposing for the ideal *polis*) would so order.

[31] ἐφιέμενοι, 434E6. Aristotle is content to define "justice" in the *Rhetoric* in terms of the (normal) result of the exercise of the virtue, making no specific reference to the intention which governs its exercise. But, of course, there is no difference of doctrine between Plato and Aristotle on this point: neither does Plato bring in explicitly the idea of intentionality into his "doing one's own" definiens, while, conversely, that idea represents one of the most fundamental elements in Aristotle's concept of moral virtue, including, of course, the virtue of justice: καὶ ἡ μὲν δικαιοσύνη ἐστὶ καθ' ἣν ὁ δίκαιος λέγεται πρακτικὸς κατὰ προαίρεσιν τοῦ δικαίου, 1134A1-2.

[32] While recasting, not just abbreviating, Plato's argument, I am keeping responsibly within the intentions of its layout in Plato's text. (1) is implicit: (if the "rulers" who are to be commissioned to judge law-suits in the Platonic πόλις (433E6-7) did not instantiate δικαιοσύνη, the inference at (3) in 433E12-434A1 would be a wild *non sequitur*. So (1) may be supplied. And it must be tied to (2) by a "because" (which is not in the text) for the same reason: were it joined only by "and," the conclusion in (3) would not follow: the fact that the aim of the judges is the one mentioned in (2) would not advance the claim made in (a part of) (3) that the achievement of this aim *is* δικαιοσύνη unless the judges' instantiation of δικαιοσύνη itself followed from (2). I offer a similar analysis of the passage in *PS*, 120-121,

[33] And so confidently that he does not put in so much as a word to justify the assumption, though it would be as plain to him as it is to us that if the assumption were not true (3) would not follow from (1) and (2), neither of which mentions "doing one's own."

one's own" by *B* and by *C* to establish the correctness of the "doing one's own" definiens of δικαιοσύνη.

Clearly, then, this definiens dovetails into the one produced by Aristotle in the *Rhetoric*. In both cases the δικαία πρᾶξις would be the one governed by the intention [34] that each of those affected by it shall "have what is his own" and neither of them shall "have what is another's." Therefore having satisfied ourselves above that in the Aristotelian definition the definiendum is used to mean not "right-eousness" but "justice," we may be equally satisfied that it is used in the same way in the Platonic. Viewed by Aristotle from the standpoint of those affected by its exercise, "justice" is defined as conduct which results in their "having their own." Viewed by Plato from the standpoint of the agent exercising it, it is defined as that "doing his own" which will have just that result. Now we can understand not only *that*, but *why*, that peculiar catch-phrase could be seriously meant as a definiens of justice, and this in spite of the fact that it only mentions "doing," instead of "having" one's own, i.e. refers directly only to duties, not to rights: the duty it has in view is *the duty of justice*—that unique, general, second order duty we are to discharge *in* each of our many particular first-order duties by so governing our conduct as to respect the rights of all whom our conduct affects.

If this argument is correct, Plato's use of the term δικαιοσύνη in the *Republic* can be explained as follows: Deprived of a special term for "justice," he is content to take a word which had this as *one* of its two senses in the language and to use it as though "justice" was simply what it meant, quietly ignoring its broader use to mean "righteousness." [35] If Plato had anticipated Aristotle's insight into the ambiguity in δικαιοσύνη, we might have had a defense of its use to mean "justice" in the *Republic*. But there is nothing in Plato's text, here or anywhere in the corpus, to show that he had noticed the two uses.[36] That being the case, he had all

---

[34] Cf. n. 31 above.

[35] Which is what Aristotle too was content to do in the *Rhetoric*. Though acutely aware in other contexts of the ambiguity in δικαιοσύνη (cf. n. 8 above), he acts here as though this is *the* sense of the term and proceeds to offer a definition which fits just that sense, blandly ignoring the other which he has recognized so fully in the opening chapters of Book V of the *N.E.*

[36] For this reason my argument that δικαιοσύνη is being used to mean "justice" in the crucial passage (443-444) which puts forward and defends the "doing one's own" definiens would not be invalidated *if* it could be shown that upon occasion Plato slips into the broader use of δικαιοσύνη in

the less reason to be self-conscious about his using δικαιοσύνη to mean "justice." This was the only use Socrates had in view in Plato's earlier dialogues when he placed δικαιοσύνη on a par with σωφροσύνη, ἀνδρεία, σοφία and ὁσιότης as one of the five "parts" of virtue.[37] This would be the use that would naturally come into the *Republic* through its Socratic portico, Book I;[38] and nothing happens thereafter to force Plato to reflect on its alternate generic use to mean "righteousness" and elicit from him a formal argument to justify his continued adherence to its narrower use. So we have good reason to concur with the traditional view that δικαιοσύνη in the *Republic* is properly translated "justice," and may now proceed with a clear conscience to investigate the theory of justice which Plato encapsulates in the definition he gives in Book IV.

## II

What is the point of the theory? Why should Plato, why should anyone, produce a theory of justice? For one or both of the two possible purposes which I shall call, following current idiom, "meta-normative" and "normative" respectively. The latter the philosopher shares with the practical moralist, the critic of politics, the social reformer. The aim here is to determine what social, economic and political rights people ought to have in consequence of the moral rights they do have. The meta-normative purpose is uniquely the philosopher's and the metaphysician's. It seeks to understand that peculiar dimension of our being which makes justice integral to our humanity—so much so that the creature we call "man" would not be fully human, if he did not have rights and duties, and therewith a concern for justice. Plato's theory has both of these purposes. I shall start with the first, giving it the lion's share of the discussion. Only towards the end will I reach the second.

Let me then go directly to the central intuition which forms the normative core of Plato's theory. This is the justice of reciprocity

the *Republic*: in the absence of a formal disambiguation of the term a certain amount of wobbling in its application would not be too surprising. I say "*If* this could be shown." It has not yet been shown, to my knowledge.

[37] *Meno* 78D-79C; *Prot.* 329C ff. And cf. *PS*, 225, n. 8, and 267.

[38] Where the species-use of δικαιοσύνη is clear (a) from Polemarchus' offering the "giving to everyone his due" definiens of the word (331E), which Socrates treats as relevant, though inadequate, and (b) from Socrates' taking πλεονεκτεῖν to be its contrary (349B ff.) which we know from Aristotle (cf. p. 4 above) to be an acceptable differentia of the species-use of δικαιοσύνη.

in the pursuit of happiness and excellence:[39] it would be just for
us to give of our best to benefit others who would be willing to
give of their best to benefit us. A rudimentary implementation of
this norm Plato had found already in that curiously abstract form
of social intercourse depicted in Book II (369A ff.), calling it
there a "πόλις," though well aware that it is only an economic
society.[40] Men's goal here is nothing higher than material well-
being, and at its lowest level—the fulfillment of the bare necessities
of life, food, clothing, shelter, and the like.[41] Yet even so it exhibits
a pattern of conduct which Plato hails as "the original principle"
of justice [42] because through what goes on here—division of labor
and exchange of goods and services on the open market—all the
participants benefit reciprocally. Each of them maximizes his
efficiency by concentrating all his energies on a single line of work
(typically a "craft" [τέχνη]) and is thus enabled to give his fellows
the best service they could expect from a person of his particular
endowment and acquired skills, reaping the benefits of the like
service from his associates. But all this happens without planned
foresight of the common good and hence with no possibility of
extending the area of mutually beneficent give-and-take into the
higher reaches of well-being.[43] For that very reason all that can be

---

[39] Here and hereafter (as also earlier, in the expansion of the "doing
one's own" definiens in n. 24) I feel free to write "happiness and excellence"
in contexts where Plato would be content to speak of εὐδαιμονία without
explicit reference to ἀρετή because for him "true" or "real" happiness
*entails* excellence. But in translations or paraphrases I shall write only
"happiness" for εὐδαιμονία in the Platonic text.

[40] He can do this by taking advantage of the ambiguity in πόλις, which
can be used to mean either *city* or *state* (and other things besides: see *LSJ
sub verbo*), making things difficult for his translators: thus Shorey starts by
translating "city" at 368E3-5, shifts to "state" at 369A1-5 and B5, then to
"city or state" at C4, finally settling down at C9 to "city" for the rest of the
passage. That Plato means no more than "city" in this whole passage is suggested by his saying that "πόλις" is "a name" for "this settlement" (ταύτῃ τῇ
συνοικίᾳ, 369C4) and it is made certain by the fact that his account of it
abstracts rigorously from all political institutions (no mention of government,
laws, courts, army, and the like).

[41] The ones which must be satisfied if man is "to exist and to live" (τοῦ
εἶναι τε καὶ τοῦ ζῆν ἕνεκα, 369D1-2); the means of their satisfaction are
"the necessaries" (τἀναγκαῖα, 373A5).

[42] ἀρχήν τε καὶ τύπον τινὰ τῆς δικαιοσύνης, 443C1.

[43] All we get at this lowest level, as Plato sees it, is a common good which,
of itself, constitutes neither happiness nor excellence (he uses neither of
these two words in his description of it) but which provides nonetheless an
indispensable component of happiness and which, moreover, requires
excellence of material craftsmanship: cf. the use of κάλλιον in 370B4 and

reached here is that low-grade communal achievement which Glaucon calls, a little too scornfully, "a city of pigs" (372D).

Over against this Plato sets another city where centrally planned pursuit of the common good governs the life of all, laying down for each a comprehensive pattern of conduct tailored to his native aptitudes, offering him whatever facilities he needs, first of all, to learn how to give his best to his fellows and then to give them that best, the same being done for everyone in the polis, so that all may be both burden-bearers and benefit-reapers, each according to his individual capacity for work and for enjoyment. This would be Plato's vision of the just πόλις. The definition of δικαιοσύνη I quoted a moment ago, "each single person's pursuing that single practice in the πόλις which his own nature best fits him to pursue"— the expansion of the "doing one's own" catch-phrase—becomes the formulaic crystallization of this vision, once it is understood that this "single service in the πόλις," though vocationally based, is not meant to be restricted to on-the-job activity but to extend over the whole of one's conduct in the πόλις, private no less than public.[44] So understood, the definition tells us that it is our supreme duty— the one that determines all others—to so conduct ourselves that each and all of our activities will contribute maximally to the happiness and excellence of our πόλις; and that if, and only if, we so conduct ourselves we shall be acting with due regard for the rights of all within the πόλις.

What then is the πόλις? I do not mean: What is its juridical

---

C3 in the justification of the division of labor and of καλῶς for the same purpose in 374A6-C2 and in the back reference to it in 394E3-4, εἷς ἕκαστος ἐν μὲν ἂν ἐπιτήδευμα καλῶς ἐπιτηδεύοι, πολλὰ δ' οὔ.

44 It is of the essence of Plato's conception of the pursuit of the good life that all persons should "have in life a single goal (σκοπὸν . . . ἐν τῷ βίῳ ἕνα) with a view to which they must do *everything* they do (οὗ στοχαζομένους δεῖ ἅπαντα πράττειν ἃ ἂν πράττωσιν) both in private and in public" (519C2-4). Those who do not have such an all-controlling purpose are ἀπαίδευτοι (519B7-8)—and there is no more damning epithet in Plato's vocabulary. Without παιδεία any virtue is a fake virtue, as is stated explicitly in the case of courage in 430B6-10: even if you do have all the right beliefs concerning what is, and is not, to be feared, but lack the proper παιδεία, your virtue will be "brutish and slavish . . . and should be called anything but 'courage'." (On this passage and the closely related one in the *Phaedo* (68D-69A) see *PS*, 137 and notes.) It follows that if you *are* "doing your own" what you do is being dictated by a purpose which commands all your energies and controls all your activities, down to the last detail. For my earlier argument for this thesis, adducing a number of other texts (the appositeness of 519C2-4 had then escaped my notice), see *PS*, 122 and 124-25 with notes.

status?—that would be another story—but: What is its status in
Plato's moral ontology? If his definition of "justice" is to keep
faith with his central intuition, the πόλις whose happiness and
excellence is the end of all just conduct within its frontiers can be
nothing but the people themselves who are its members—all of them
in all of their institutionalized interrelations.[45] I contend that this
is all the πόλις is for Plato. I must argue for this claim, for it has
often been denied. Grote denied it flatly over a century ago in his
monumental book on Plato. Let me quote him:

> Plato announces explicitly the purpose of all his arrangements: to
> obtain happiness for the whole city: by which he means, not happiness
> for the greatest number of individuals, but for the abstract unity called
> the City, supposed to be capable of happiness or misery, apart from the
> individuals, many or few, composing it.[46]

A similar thesis has been strongly affirmed in our time by Sir
Karl Popper [47] in his *Open Society and its Enemies*.[48] Assuring us
(169) that

> Plato says frequently that what he is aiming at is neither the happiness
> of individuals nor that of any particular class in the state, but only the
> happiness of the whole,[49]

---

[45] I say "all" of those interrelations, because for Plato the πόλις is coex-
tensive with all the associations of its members, be they economic, familial,
educational, recreational, cultural, or religious, no less than that unique
association for which the term "political" would be ordinarily reserved, i.e.
the one which in a given territorial area (a) exercises supreme control over
the use of physical coercion, and (b) maintains a legal order.

[46] *Plato and the Other Companions of Socrates* (London, 1888), vol. 4, 139,
(The first, three-volume, edition had appeared in 1865).

[47] Also, somewhat less strongly by Cross and Woozley: they claim that for
Plato "the state is itself an individual" (76), a "super-individual" (132),
but that this is only an *implication* of Plato's explicit doctrines, never
"clearly recognized" (132) by Plato, and not a consistently sustained
implication (78, 132). My criticism of this interpretation will be directed
exclusively to the full-strength form in which it is expounded by Grote and
Popper.

[48] Cf n. 2 above, and Appendix A.

[49] Taking the cited statement at face value, and ignoring for the moment
the fact that "the whole" is meant to be a stand-in for a disputed entity
(the "super-individual"), the statement would be quite innocuous, except in
one special case—the crucial one—where "the happiness of individuals"
is that of *all* the individuals who compose the whole. In any other case
(including, not least of all, the one most likely to come to mind, where
"the happiness of individuals" is construed in terms of the Benthamite
formula used by Grote in the statement cited from him above, "happiness
for the greatest number," and "greatest" could stand for some number

Popper calls this "whole" a "super-individual," [50] to indicate that it is distinct from any and all of the individuals who compose it and superior to each and all of them in value.[51]

Now I am not going to suggest that this view is a whole-cloth fabrication. A great thinker who is also a great stylist must be held co-responsible for the deeper misunderstandings of his text. Certainly there are passages which spin cloth for Grote and Popper.[52] To go through them and ponder their precise import would call for another paper. Fortunately there is no need to do this here. The falsehood of the imputation can be established without having to go so far afield. Let me focus on the very passage to which Grote refers in the lines I quoted from him, sc. to that long paragraph near the very start of Book IV where Plato speaks of "creating the happy πόλις" (τὴν εὐδαίμονα πλάττομεν πόλιν, 420C3). What he means by this phrase becomes clearer in his repeated references to the happiness of "the whole πόλις," which contrast it invariably with the happiness of a particular group within the πόλις—never with that of all the people in the πόλις.[53] What we are told in the

short of the full totality), what Popper says would be entirely correct. What is surprising is that it should pass muster for the crucial case even in the eyes of so lucid a thinker and careful reader of Plato's text as Richard Robinson. (Cf. the first of the two quotations from him under (2) in the Appendix A below.)

[50] P. 76; also "a kind of super-organism" (79).

[51] The second of these allegations is easily documented, though only by filling out the ellipses which Popper (usually an exact writer) allows himself freely in this case: "the individual is lower than the state" (79); "the state . . . must be placed higher than the individual" (76). In the case of the former I cannot recall any passage in which the "super-individual" is explicitly contrasted with all of the people who compose it (though often enough with unquantified "individuals") but the contrast is unambiguously implied by the choice of the term "super-individual," on the safe assumption that this could hardly be meant to be rhetorical bombast devoid of exact philosophical import, as it would be if it were simply meant to name the totality of individuals in their multiple inter-relations.

[52] Many of them are reviewed and their alleged support of the ascription of the "super-individual" view to Plato is rebutted in Jerry Neu's paper, "Plato's Analogy of State and Individual," Philosophy 46 (1971), 238-54. Particularly valuable is his terse identification (245 and notes, especially n. 21) of the misunderstanding of Platonic ontology ("misplaced degrees-of-reality theory") incurred in Popper's allegation (79-80) that for Plato the state has greater "reality" than its citizens, and is itself "the perfect individual" of which the individual citizen is "a kind of imperfect copy"—mistakes which R. B. Levinson's critique (pp. 518 ff. of the work cited in Appendix A below) had failed to spot.

[53] ἕν τι ἔθνος vs. ὅλη ἡ πόλις, 420B6-7; ὀλίγους . . . τινὰς vs. ὅλην, C3-4; making the members of some particular trade μακαρίους vs. contriving that

above quotation from Popper Plato "says frequently," he never says even once for the crucial case where "the happiness of individuals" is that of *all* the individuals in the state: in none of them does Plato draw that contrast at all. To be sure, there is a passage— just one in the entire Platonic corpus, to my knowledge—where Plato does, in effect, compare the happiness of the whole πόλις with that of all the people who compose it; and it is instructive to test the Grote-Popper hypothesis against it: Plato is here considering what would happen if all the subgroups in the polis could be given their heart's desire of self-indulgent happiness in childish disregard of the consequences for the performance of their duties and therewith for the happiness of everyone else:

> Don't require us to give the guardians the sort of happiness that would make them anything but guardians. For in the same way we could dress up the farmers in gorgeous robes and deck them out with gold, and tell them to work the land at their pleasure; and we could have the potters too recline in banquet-couches, left to right, boozing and feasting, with their potter's wheel at their side to potter with when they are so disposed; and all the others too we could make happy in the same fashion, so that indeed the whole city might be happy (ἵνα δὴ ὅλη ἡ πόλις εὐδαιμονῇ), 420D5-E7 (translation adapted from Shorey's).

Here the happiness of the whole πόλις is not treated as something distinct from the happiness of the citizens; it is collapsed with theirs. The fact that the hypothesis is counterfactual—it would turn the πόλις into an amusement-park, a "country-fair" (ὥσπερ ἐν πανηγύρει, 421B2), and the result would be disastrous *un*happiness—in no way affects the point at issue, which is that *if* all the people in the πόλις could be made happy in this crazy way then the whole πόλις would *be* happy.

But there is another passage which provides stronger evidence for my case, for it distinctly implies, as this one perhaps does not, the very contrary of what Plato has been supposed to have said "frequently." When the philosophers are sentenced to a fifteen-

---

ὅλη ἡ πόλις εὐδαιμονῇ, E1-7; πλείστη εὐδαιμονία for the guardians *or* for the whole πόλις, 421B5-7; ἕν τι γένος *vs.* ἐν ὅλῃ τῇ πόλει, 519E2-3. The Cross-Woozley handling of these passages is unobjectionable. Here is their excellent gloss on the first of them:

> "... the aim is to provide the conditions of happiness, not for one class (ἔθνος), but for the city as a whole. Whether or not this entails the concept of a city as an entity over and above the individuals who comprise it (and the analogy of the statue in 420C-D perhaps suggests that it does not), at least it entails the idea of a man being prepared to subordinate his own interests to those of others" (97).

year exile from their intellectual paradise to do a stint of service in
the Cave, this is how Socrates explains the rationale of the verdict
(519E1-520A2):

> You have forgotten, my friend, that it is not the law's concern to secure
> superior happiness for a single class in the state, but to contrive this [54]
> in the whole πόλις,[55] harmonizing the citizens by persuasion and com-
> pulsion, making them impart to *one another* the benefit which each of
> them can bring to the community (ποιῶν μεταδιδόναι ἀλλήλοις τῆς
> ὠφελίας ἥν ἂν ἕκαστοι τὸ κοινὸν δυνατοὶ ὦσιν ὠφελεῖν).

What is described in the second dependent clause of the citation
as "contriving this [superior happiness] in the whole πόλις," is
redescribed in the terminal clause as the citizens' "imparting *to
one another* the benefit which each can bring to the community."
Thus for them to "impart benefit to the community" (τὸ κοινὸν
ὠφελεῖν) *is* to "impart benefit to one another"; they, and they
alone, are the beneficiary; the well-being of the πόλις is theirs.[56]
How Grote, splendid Hellenist and exceedingly close student of the
*Republic* that he was, could have missed the import of this passage,
must remain a mystery. How Popper missed it, though also mysterious, becomes a little less so, when we notice that when he
quotes this passage the crucial words "to one another" drop out of
his translation.[57] When put back where they should be—and where

---

54 I.e. superlative well-being. Here I disagree with Shorey's gloss on
519E3: he says that the reference of "this" is "happiness, not of course
exceptional happiness." When he wrote that "of course" Shorey must have
forgotten that in his translation of 420B6-7 he had resolved the same ambiguity of reference in the opposite way (writing "the greatest possible
happiness of the city as a whole" for ὅτι μάλιστα ὅλη ἡ πόλις [διαφερόντως
εὐδαίμων ἔσται]). It would make as good sense to say that the whole πόλις
is "exceptionally" happy as to say this of a particular class within it, so
long as the referents of the comparison are appropriately different (other
cities, in one case; other classes within the same city, in the other).

55 ἐν ὅλῃ τῇ πόλει. The force of the preposition is lost in some translations
of the phrase (Cornford: "of the commonwealth as a whole"; Bloom: "for
the whole city"). The phrase is faithfully rendered, as above, in Lindsay,
Shorey, Robin.

56 That is why he feels free to speak of this, indifferently, as
(a) happiness "in" the πόλις (ἐν τῇ πόλει, 519E3), or
(b) happiness "for" it (εἰ πλείστη εὐδαιμονία ἐκείνη ἐγγίγνεται, (421B6-7), or
(c) happiness "of" the πόλις (τὴν εὐδαιμονίαν ... τοῦ τε ἀνδρὸς καὶ τῆς
πόλεως, 566D5).
Since it is the happiness of the persons who compose the city, it may be
described either literally, as in (a), i.e. as something that happens *within*
it, or a little more freely in (b) and in (c) as happiness "for" or "of" the city.

57 This is how he translates (80) 519E5-520A1: "It makes them all share
in whatever benefit each of them can contribute to the community".

they are in all of the other translations I have consulted,[58] with
the single exception of Cornford's,[59] on which Popper's seems
modelled [60]—they leave no reasonable grounds for doubt on the
point at issue. They show directly that contribution to the happiness of one's πόλις means for Plato contribution to the happiness
of everyone within the network of interrelations which bind the
life of everyone in the πόλις to the life of everyone else.

So my interpretation of the "doing one's own" definiens of
"justice" keeps well in line with what I called the "central intuition" in Plato's theory. The duty of justice it defines is fulfilled
in doing one's best to contribute to the happiness and excellence
of everyone in the πόλις, and to that alone.

If we did fulfil this duty could we ourselves count on equal
treatment? The question would leap to the mind of Plato's reader
then, no less than it does now, indeed then more than now, for the
linguistic bond of justice with equality was even closer for the
Greeks than it is for us: τὸ ἴσον, ἰσότης, would be the very words to
which they would turn for a natural, unstrained, one-word variant
for τὸ δίκαιον, δικαιοσύνη.[61] This is what leads Aristotle to declare
that "justice *is* equality, as all men think even apart from argu-

---

In this rendering Plato's statement would not be inconsistent with Popper's
interpretation: It would not forbid his taking "the community" (τὸ κοινόν)
here to mean the "super-individual," understanding Plato to be saying that
each of the citizens is to bring his contributions to the "super-individual"
and receive in turn *some* share in the riches pouring in to *it*.

[58] Schleiermacher-Kurz, Lindsay, Shorey, Robin, Bloom. Also Jowett
(but in the revised [4th, 1953] edition Jowett's "one another" was changed
to "others"—why?).

[59] Which reads, *"making them share whatever benefits each* class *can contribute* to the common good." (I have italicized the words which recur in
Popper's translation, cited in n. 57 above). This translation is even less exact
than Popper's: ἕκαστοι, whose reference is clearly to τοὺς πολίτας in the
preceding line, becomes "each class": and "the common good" for τὸ κοινόν
is unnecessarily free.

[60] The recurrence in Popper's of the words I have italicized in my quotation of Cornford's in the preceding note makes this a virtual certainty. But
the vital blemish—the omission of "with one another" after "share" in each
of the two translations—cannot be explained by supposing that Popper was
following Cornford's blindly: He corrected inexactness in Cornford at two
other points in this sentence.

[61] For such uses of ἴσος see the examples in LSJ, *s.v.* ἴσος (sense B, I, 2)
and in *PS*, 184, n. 78 *sub fin.* An earlier example not cited by either is
Theognis 543-44:

χρή με παρὰ στάθμην καὶ γνώμονα τήνδε δικάσαι,
Κύρνε, δίκην, ἴσόν τ' ἀμφοτέροισιν δόμεν.

ment." [62] And this is certainly how Plato himself understands the common view: both Socrates and Callicles in the *Gorgias*,[63] and then again Glaucon at the start of Book II of the *Republic* [64] take it for granted that for the public at large "justice" and "equality"—τὸ δίκαιον and τὸ ἴσον—can be used interchangeably. What then is Plato's answer to my question? At first sight there seems to be none: no word for "equality" gets into the text of Books IV and V where he propounds, defends and applies his definition of "justice," nor yet in any later book in this extensive dialogue, except in VIII, in his brush with democracy, where he handles the word brusquely in non-committal reportage,[65] or wry epigram,[66] or poison-dipped gibes,[67] without a moment's pause to pick it up and probe its meaning. Does this betray evasiveness or uncertainty in his attitude to equality? By no means. Plato knows his own mind well and manages to speak it forcefully in spite of a defective vocabulary, though the message would have been clearer with the right words than it is now without them. The one he needed most urgently at this point is Greek for "impartiality": for this there is only ἰσότης, and to recognize this use of ἰσότης you would have to distinguish *formal* from *substantive* equality,[68] *equal regard for*

---

[62] Cited in n. 11 above. The sense would be the same if we translated ἄνευ λόγου "apart from theory."

[63] First Callicles (483C5 and 484A1), then Socrates (488E-489A) use τὸ ἴσον ἔχειν to express the opposite of ἀδικεῖν (= πλέον ἔχειν). This is one of the very few points on which the adversaries agree without argument.

[64] See the reference to 359C6 on p. 8 above.

[65] Democracy is said to come about "when the poor, winning out, kill some of the other party, expel others, and *give an equal share* (ἐξ ... ἴσου μεταδῶσι) *of the constitution and the offices to the rest, making most of the appointments to office by lot*" (557A)—the italicized clauses are a neutral, non-controversial description of a democratic regime, which would be as acceptable to democrats as to their adversaries: ἐξ ἴσου μεταδιδόναι (or μετέχειν) τῆς πολιτείας would be a standard way of referring to the uniquely democratic allocation of civic rights; see e.g. the references given in *PS*, notes to 193-94, and cf. 174, n. 41.

[66] 558C5-6.

[67] 562D-E (where ὁμοίους, ὅμοιον are being used as variants for ἴσους, ἴσον: cf. ἐξισοῦσθαι, 563A1); 563B7-9. There is cheap exaggeration in these two passages, and the last plays to the male chauvinist gallery in a way which is surprising to say the least after Plato's bold words on the emancipation of women in Book V. Popper is perfectly right in speaking of these passages as "abusive attack on democracy," "cheap cracks," 254.

[68] To say this is not to imply that if you had not drawn that distinction (or an equivalent one) you could not have used ἴσος, ἰσότης to mean "impartial," "impartiality." To follow a rule of language one does not have to know the rule, still less to know that one is following it in a particular case:

*rights* from *regard for equal rights* [69]—a distinction that had yet to be made, and was never made in the classical period: it is still missing in Aristotle when he links up τὸ δίκαιον with τὸ ἴσον in the *Nicomachean Ethics*.[70] I want to argue that nevertheless there is no wobbling or confusion in Plato's attitude to impartiality; his moral commitment to it is firm and fiercely uncompromising.

We see this in the treatment he prescribes for that class to which he was most strongly tempted to be partial: his own. Every secular aristocracy known to man has used its power to corner for itself privileged wealth, sex, and leisure. Plato's aristocracy is to have absolute control of the coercive apparatus of the state [71] and is, therefore, able to grab and keep as much of each of these three

---

cf. *PS*, 241, n. 53. Thus Plato found it natural to speak of an *impartial* judge as an "equal" one (*Laws* 957C, τὸν μέλλοντα δικαστὴν ἴσον γενέσθαι . . .) though he had never *recognized* in his writings that ἴσος can be used to mean just that.

[69] The first corresponds to *formal* justice, which is a second-order component of justice, consisting in respect for the second-order right to have all of one's substantive rights respected. (Cf. my "Justice and Equality" (cited in n. 20 above), 55.) The difference between formal and substantive equality becomes clearer if one reflects on the fact that, within wide limits, they are independent variables. Thus formal equality comports with extreme variations in substantive equality: if A is a slave and B a citizen, then, so far as legal justice is concerned, formal equality will be satisfied if and only if each of the vast inequalities in their legal rights is strictly enforced. Conversely, substantive equality does not entail formal equality. Thus the substantive right which persons of all colors have to "the equal protection of the laws" under the constitution of the United States may be nullified by a racist law-enforcement officer who thumbs his nose at formal equality. Plato's stand on equality, as I shall be arguing, could be lucidly described as full commitment to formal equality, unaccompanied by any commitment to substantive equality, though without going to the other extreme: no commitment to substantive *in*equality either.

[70] The best he can do towards locating the idea of impartiality on his conceptual map is to note that that what he calls "commutative" justice is not "geometrical," but "arithmetical," equality (*N.E.* 1131B32 ff.) This is not nearly good enough, since as he (and others) use "arithmetical" equality it is in the first instance a concept of *substantive* equality, referring primarily to those equal rights of citizenship which are characteristic of the democratic constitution. What he needs (and fails) to locate is that particular species of "arithmetical" equality which could be shared by both proponents and opponents of democratic equality.

[71] Though this is, of course, built into the political structure of the *Republic* (the military, the only arms-bearing group, in the πόλις, are under the sole control of the philosophers), one is apt to forget it, because references to internal repression or compulsion are so rare: 415E 1-2 is the clearest; and Professor Michael Rohr has pointed out to me the implied use of force in 465A8-9.

kinds of goodies as it wants.[72] But Plato decrees that the rulers are to have not more, but less, of each than will their subjects. Private property will be denied the Guardians absolutely.[73] Like Lenin's first soviet they are to subsist on workingmen's wages.[74] Private family will be also denied them; during long stretches of their adult lives—thirty-five for men, twenty for women—they must endure the misery of celibacy relieved at infrequent intervals [75] by the bleak gratifications of reproductive service to the state.[76] And for fifteen years they must also renounce what Plato thinks they would covet most of all [77]—the chance to do full-time intellectual work. Historians tell us that no ruling class has ever surrendered of its own accord functionless privilege it had power to keep. When Plato insists that his philosophers submit to these massive renunciations simply because those privileges would be socially unfunctional and counterfunctional [78] he declares unmistakably his commitment to impartiality: his actions speak more loudly than would words.

---

[72] Plato calls this to our attention. He has Adeimantus ask how Socrates could justify the denial of property to the guardians when "the πόλις really belongs to them." Socrates recalls this later on (466A): "Do you remember that someone reproached us earlier for not making the guardians happy, who with power to have all the property of the citizens (οἷς ἐξὸν πάντα ἔχειν τὰ τῶν πολιτῶν) were to have no property (οὐδὲν ἔχοιεν)?"

[73] 416D-420A.

[74] παρὰ τῶν ἄλλων τροφὴν λαμβάνοντας, μισθὸν τῆς φυλακῆς, 464C1-2.

[75] Just when these are to come is not stated. They may all fall within the duration of an annual festival, as Cornford conjectures (op. cit., 159, n. 2). The essential constraint is that the number of the occasions on which intercourse is permitted will be just sufficient to impregnate all the women who are due to bear children during a given year.

[76] It may be objected that Plato, a homosexual (cf. PS, 25, n. 74), would not consider this deprivation particularly burdensome. The objection has no force: the proposals have in view a constituency within which the desire for heterosexual intimacy is widely distributed at the usual pitch of intensity. Otherwise, the prospect of more frequent stud-service (460B) and of milder sexual liberties with partners of both sexes (466C1-3) would not be the incentives to martial valor which they are obviously meant to be. (On the difference between 460B and 466C1-3 conflated by Popper [150-51] as by others, see PS, 22, n. 65).

[77] Judging from the earnestness of his apologia for the justice of the infliction of this hardship on the philosophers (519D-521B).

[78] Obviously so in the case of the third (on the implied assumption that the job of government would not be done as well if relegated to a non-philosophical bureaucracy), and certainly so in the case of the first two as well (on the explicit assumption that private property and private family would be morally corrupting: cf. n. 85 below).

And he does more: he discloses at the same time the principle of
the allocation of substantive rights entailed by his conception of
justice—a principle which otherwise we would not have known, for
he never spells it out, and we could not have squeezed it out of his
central intuition of reciprocity in the pursuit of happiness. For
all this says is that everyone will behave justly if, and only if, he
so conducts himself as to maximize his individual contribution to
the common happiness; and that if he so behaves, he may be
assured that he too will have *a* share in the collective product of the
like contributions of others. How big will be *his* share relatively to
that of others it does not say. Plato never tackles this question in
the *Republic*. And if we had had to guess our way to his answer
without further directions from him, we would have been likely to
guess wrong: the plausible, indeed the only reasonable, inference
would have been that his rule of distributive justice is contained in
the doctrine of "proportional" equality [79] with which Plato flirted
both before and in the *Republic*, and was eventually to marry in
the *Laws*. He alludes to it in the *Gorgias* under the caption of
"geometrical" equality.[80] He makes momentary use of it in Book
VIII of the *Republic*, leaning on it there for the effect of the quip
about democracy "distributing a sort of equality to equals and
unequals alike" (558C).[81] And he praises it to the skies in the
*Laws*, declaring there that "to distribute more to the greater
(merit), less to the lesser" [82] would be "always precisely what
constitutes political justice" [83] and natural, divinely ordained,

---

[79] Popular among fourth-century conservatives: Isocrates, *Nicocles*, 15
(cited in n. 89 below), and *Areopagiticus* 21-22 (who speaks of it as κατ'
ἀξίαν τιμᾶν ἕκαστον); Aristotle, *Nic. Eth.* 1131A30 ff. (cf. n. 12 above), and
*Pol.* 1280A9 ff. and 1301A26 ff.

[80] 508A6-7, where "geometrical equality" is identified with δικαιοσύνη
in opposition to the πλεονεξία advocated by Callicles. For comment see
E. R. Dodds, *Plato, Gorgias* (Oxford, 1959), 339-40; and *PS*, 195, n. 119.

[81] Cf. my comment on this in *PS*, 194.

[82] 757C1-6, τῷ γὰρ μείζονι πλείω, τῷ δ' ἐλάττονι σμικρότερα νέμει ..., τὸ
πρέπον ἑκατέροις ἀπονέμει κατὰ λόγον.

[83] 757C6-7, ἔστι γὰρ δήπου καὶ τὸ πολιτικὸν ἡμῖν ἀεὶ τοῦτ' αὐτὸ τὸ δίκαιον.
The significance of the καί, lost in some translations, but preserved in
A. E. Taylor's (otherwise uncomfortably inflated) rendering, "this sheer
justice is always also the statesmanlike policy," I take to be: this "proportional" (κατὰ λόγον, 757B5-6) allocation, which is sanctioned by both God
(Διὸς κρίσις, B7) and nature (πρὸς τὴν αὐτῶν φύσιν ἑκατέρῳ, C3), is not only
ideally best ("the truest and best," B6), but *also* practicable (for the second-
best state envisaged in the *Laws*) and thus the statesmanlike one (πολιτικόν,
C6). Plato's enthusiasm for "proportional" equality here makes him overstate

justice to boot. But when he comes to work out the allocation of rights in the central books of the *Republic* he cold-shoulders it: [84] not even a remote allusion to proportional equality there, and for good reason: it would have implied that the Guardians, who do the most for the πόλις, have a right to all of its largest rewards, while, as we have seen, Plato repeatedly mandates not bigger and juicier plums for the biggest contributors, but smaller and drier ones, hygienic prunes instead of hedonic plums.[85]

If Plato had undertaken to make "proportional" equality the central, instead of a merely tangential, principle of distributive justice in the *Republic*, he would have discovered how limited are its uses for this purpose. It works, so far as it does work, only for *socially distributable* compensations. It cannot regulate the greatest by far of the rewards vouchsafed to the philosophers—the one which comes to them through their very love of "Justice itself," in their mystical communion with the Form,[86] and in the effect this has on their own soul: the incarnation of the eternal harmony in the tissues of their psyche.[87] The question of anyone's distribut-

---

its validity. No sooner has he said that this *is* political justice than he has to backtrack and admit (757D6 ff.) that the other "equality," the mechanical or arithmetical one (757B4-5), must also be allowed a place, regrettably so, "for it breaks off from the correct justice when it occurs" (παρὰ δίκην τὴν ὀρθήν ἐστι παρατεθραυμένον, 757E2).

[84] The significance of this fact seems to have gone unnoticed in the scholarly literature, where he is regularly cited as upholding the principle of "proportional" equality in the *Republic* on the strength of 558C: Barker, *op. cit.*, 189, n. 2; K. Bringmann, *Studien zu den politischen Ideen des Isokrates* (*Hypomnemata*, No. 14, 1965), 86; R. Maurer, *Platons "Staat" und die Demokratie* (Berlin, 1970), 75 ff. My own comment on 558C in *PS*, 194 (in the essay, *Isonomia Politike*, originally published in 1964) also misses this point.

[85] Considerations of political hygiene decide the economic and sexual deprivations inflicted on the Guardians: if they were allowed private property they would become "hateful masters, instead of allies, to the other citizens" (417A-B); and if allowed the personal bonds engendered by private family (and also, presumably, extra-marital sexual attachments) the total emotional identification with the πόλις would be fractured (462A-E). Popper's dictum that for Plato "morality is nothing but political hygiene" (107: see my comment, *PS*, 14-15) is false only because of its wild overstatement; there is indeed a large dose of political hygiene in the morality of the *Republic*.

[86] See *PS*, 52-53 and 54-56. And cf. n. 109 below.

[87] 500C2-D1:
Viewing and contemplating that which is ordered and forever invariant . . . (will not the philosopher) imitate it and, so far as possible, assimilate itself to it? Or do you think it would be possible not to imitate that with which one holds loving converse? . . . So the philosopher, consorting with the divine and the harmonious, will himself become divine and harmonious so far as this is possible for man.

ing this to anyone does not arise: it is that reward of virtue which is virtue itself. As to distributable rewards, honor is the one that can, and will, be shared out to the philosophers in quantities worthy of their matchless contribution; they will be billionaires of honor in the Platonic state.[88] But in respect of other kinds of socially distributable goods Platonic justice would flout "proportional" equality. It would outrage Isocrates [89] and Co. by giving less of some of the major means of happiness to those who give the πόλις more. That is why I have been suggesting that to reach the general principle of rights-allocation in the *Republic* we should follow him in forgetting all about "proportional" equality. His unstated, but firmly followed, rule is that each has a right to those, and only those, socially distributable benefits which will maximize his contribution, regardless of the ratio which the value of services rendered bears to that of benefits received. This model of just distribution would not require us to make output to individuals proportionate to the value of their input. Quite the contrary: it would constrain us to curtail rights when leaner rations are more likely to yield better service.

Given this model, and the collateral assumptions which Plato makes about what is best done by whom, the allocation of rights which produces the social structure of the rationally ordered πόλις of Plato's vision becomes completely lucid: both its political inequalities, which are catastrophic, and its socio-economic equalities, which are substantial, become intelligible without any need to refer to "proportional" equality at all. The right to participate in the functions of government—in any such function whatsoever, be it executive, deliberative, legislative, judicial, electoral or administrative—is denied absolutely to the populace; it is handed over *in toto* to a tiny minority of intellectuals [90] simply and solely because this function, like every social function, belongs of right

---

[88] Quasi-divine honors will be accorded to them:
  And the state shall establish public memorials and sacrifices for them as to divinities if the Pythian oracle approves or, if not, as divine and godlike men. (540B7-C2 in Shorey's translation).

[89] Isocrates' account of the principle of proportional equality:
  ... make the largest distribution to the best, the next largest to the next best, and in the same proportion to the third, fourth, and so on (*Nicocles* 15).

[90] τῷ σμικροτάτῳ ἔθνει—so small that there would be "many more" coppersmiths than Guardians in the πόλις (428D11-E7).

to those who can do it best, and Plato is persuaded that the philos-ophers would do it best and better without than with participation by the governed. The question of making government the exclusive prerogative of the philosophers as a reward for their preeminent virtue does not arise; if it did, the answer would be in reverse: because they are so virtuous they can be expected to make bigger sacrifices in personal happiness for the common good, the biggest of them being the very exercise of the right to govern, which Plato thinks a painful bore. And to the question of allowing them greater liberty as a reward for virtue, the answer would be the same: in respect of personal liberty they are not to be better off, but worse off, than the producers. If a philosopher were to voice a forbidden thought [91] or sport a deviant haircut, he would be censured more severely than would others lower down the social scale who do not have to carry so heavy a burden of exemplary virtue. Similarly in the economic area the design of rights is strictly functional, and yields, on one hand, the radical equality of monastic poverty for the philosophers and, on the other, a sharp reduction of inequality in the distribution of wealth among its producers: neither opulence nor indigence will be allowed them because either deviation from the norm of modest sufficiency would be detrimental to good craftsmanship. [92]

---

[91] Popper is surely right in rejecting the claim that Plato believed in free speech for the upper classes (270): free speech would be meaningless unless it included the liberty to advocate unorthodox views (not merely to voice them non-commitally in argument) and to do so in public forums (not merely in camera). But Popper goes too far in maintaining (loc. cit.) that Plato would not even permit the philosophers free discussion among them-selves. For this there is no positive evidence whatever, and it would take evidence of the most unambiguous kind to convince us that Plato would deny to his philosophers the lifeblood of philosophical inquiry which courses through his own dialogues.

[92] 421C-E. To realize how drastic would be the curtailment of inequalities in income in the Platonic πόλις in contrast to the status quo, one should remember that Plato envisages an economy of self-employed farmers and craftsmen (working, presumably, with individually owned slaves), while the economic inequalities of contemporary Athens were due mainly to the existence of an entrepreneurial class and, even more, to a class of absentee land-owners and rentiers living on inherited wealth, like Callias, reputed to be the richest man in Athens; we may form some idea of his income from the fact that Nikias, who was not particularly famous for his wealth, was still rich enough to own a thousand slaves he hired out at an obol a day to a concessionaire at the silver mines at Laureion (Xenophon, Poroi 4, 14; the same passage mentions two other Athenian gentlemen who hired out respec-tively 600 and 300 slaves to mine operators).

## III

So we would be misdescribing Plato's view if we were to say with Popper that for Plato "justice meant inequality." [93] Plato never said anything to imply this. What he would have said if required to put his view into that kind of language is that justice could mean either equality or inequality, depending on which of the two would be most conducive to "doing one's own." The greatest interest of his theory for the student of the spectrum of variations in philosophical concepts of justice is that here, if anywhere in western thought, we have the chance to see what the link of justice with equality would look like if it were reduced to the equal right to functional reciprocity, on one hand,[94] and to formal equality, on the other. We would miss our chance if we construed Plato as a root-and-branch adversary of equality, for we would then be, in effect, denying him any concept of justice at all: Without formal equality at the very least, justice would be as much of a contradiction as would triangularity without angularity. And though formal equality is, tautologously, a formal principle, adherence to it is no formality. The moral dimension of the principle is impartiality, and I have been at pains to underline the sincerity of Plato's commitment to this exacting and costly virtue. Only when we have realized that to this extent Plato is at one with us—he has concern, burning concern, for justice, not for some artifact of his own invention which he chooses to name "justice"—can we measure the distance which separates his justice from ours because of the difference in our respective convictions on the relation of justice to substantive equality.

---

[93] "Why did Plato claim, in the *Republic*, that justice meant inequality if, in general usage, it meant equality?" (92).

[94] The rule of distributive justice mentioned on p. 24 above—"that each has a right to those, and only those, socially distributable benefits which will maximize his contribution"—defines an *equal* right, entailing equal treatment for all members of the polis in that their function is their sole title to the benefits distributed within the polis. Hence all are assured that all contributions of equal value will be equally rewarded, and that their individual reward, be it equal or unequal to that of others, will be fixed on the scale which is most likely to elicit from each maximal contribution to the happiness and excellence of the polis—that is to say (as I have argued on pp. 14-18 above), the happiness and excellence of every member of the polis, including their own.

That distance is greatest for those committed to the liberal view of
justice. Here let me speak for myself: Plato's principle of the
justice of reciprocity in the pursuit of happiness and excellence I
would, of course, accept. But all rights generated by that principle
I would subordinate to those generated by the principle of equal
human dignity. And these are strictly equal: inhering in man's
humanity,[95] not in his excellence or productivity, they are untouched by variations in excellence or productivity. Not that
I would be less concerned for high achievement than was Plato,
but that my very concern for this derives from my concern for
humanity. When I ask: "What is excellence for? What is science
for, and art, and every other value-creating form of human endeavor?", I can only answer: For the sake of human beings—
those now living and those yet unborn—whose lives may be made
thereby more secure and more free, may be ennobled and en-
riched. In this capacity—as, in Kant's phrase, ends-in-themselves [96]
and, therefore, as the ends for which all the gains of civilization
are, in the last analysis, mere means—human individuals are all
absolutely equal and are so recognized in the precepts of morality [97]
and in democratic law. The allocation of differential rights must,
therefore, start from a base of substantive equality, taking that as
the rockbottom foundation of all other rights. Plato's scheme has no
such base. Its substantive differentials are bottomless. He therefore

---

[95] In Locke's phrase, "they belong to men as men, and not as members of
society" (Two Treatises on Civil Government, II, 14). He says this of (the
right to) "truth and keeping of faith"; but he would certainly affirm it of all
those rights which he deems "inalienable" and "imprescriptible."

[96] See Appendix B.

[97] This fundamental point is insufficiently stressed—seldom even mentioned—in discussions of human equality (in the moral, not the biological,
import of this notion). It is particularly relevant to a critique of Plato, who
not only fails to recognize that our common moral precepts define constraints
on conduct which are equally binding on all (as they must, to be equally
protective of all), but, in effect, denies this presupposition in his discussion
of the "noble lie": the obligation to speak the truth does not rest equally
on all; it holds for private citizens addressing rulers, but not reciprocally
(389B, 414 ff.): the fact that the asymmetry is rationalized (lying is permitted only for the good of those lied to, and only the rulers have knowledge of
the good) does not mitigate the inequality but, on the contrary, enforces it.
Popper's charge that "Plato established for his philosopher kings the duty
and privilege of using lies and deceit for the benefit of the city" (328) is
exactly correct. Levinson's reply (op. cit., 435) concedes the charge of
"lying propaganda"; the defense he offers—that there is "some truth" in
the Platonic "noble lie"—is beside the point.

accepts as entirely just inequalities entailing personal subjection so extreme as to be unparalleled in Greek experience, except in slavery; and Plato does not hesitate to depict it as idealized slavery.

He does so late in Book IX (590C2-D6) in one of the least noticed passages in the *Republic*,[98] though it is surely one of the most revealing:

> Why do you think the condition of the manual laborer is despised? [99] Is it for any reason other than this: when one has by nature a feeble portion of the best part [of the soul] (i.e. reason), he cannot rule the brood of beasts within him, but can only serve them and learn to flatter them?...
>
> Therefore, that he too may be ruled in like manner as the best man, we say that he ought to be the slave [100] of that best man who has the

---

[98] 590C2-591A3. I have referred to this passage in my "Slavery in Plato's Thought" (*PS*, 151 and n. 17, where I comment on the earlier use of this passage by B. Bosanquet) and then again in my essay on Platonic Love (*PS*, 13 and n. 34) and, more briefly, in other essays. It is cited to good effect by J. Neu on p. 248 of his paper (cited in n. 52 above); and there are valuable notes on the passage in Shorey's translation. I can recall no reference to it in many of the discussions of Platonic justice to which it would be highly germane—Popper, Barker, Murphy (*Interpretation of Plato's "Republic"* (Oxford, 1951)), Cross and Woozley—but cannot check for lack of an *index locorum* in any of these books except Popper's which does *not* list it in its index. There is no reference to it in G. R. Morrow, *Plato's Cretan City* (Princeton, 1960). None in L. G. Versenyi, "Plato and his Liberal Opponents," *Philosophy* 46 (1971), 222-237, who reproduces its main ideas *in propria persona* ("The freedom of the natural slave, the man so devoid of a knowledge of what is good for him that he is incapable of ruling himself for his own good, is not good for the slave. For his own good, he should be ruled, absolutely, by someone who knows" (232)).

[99] "Reproach" in Lindsay's and Shorey's translations of ὄνειδος is surely wrong: it would convey the implication that manual labor is *morally* discreditable, which, of course, is not what Plato means here, and is not necessarily contained in the proper connotation of ὄνειδος (to be sure, this is normally used to mean "reproach, censure"; but it can also be used more loosely to cover unfavorable response [elicited by non-moral, as well as by moral, properties]). Cornford's rendering of ὄνειδος φέρει "discredited as debasing," gets the sense right, but only by over-translating. With ὄνειδος φέρει here about "banausic" occupations cf. ἐπίρρητοί... εἰσι in Xenophon, *Oec.* 4, 2-3, where the reason offered is that these employments make bodies "more womanish" and *thereby* make the souls "feebler" (a common sentiment: for Plato's version of it see 495D-E, with Adam's and Shorey's notes *ad loc.*), while Plato's point here is that the intellectual deficiency in the "slave's" congenital endowment (his "nature": φύσει ἔχει, 590C3, to be compared with φύσις in 433A6) is the basic (and unavoidable) cause of his moral debility.

[100] δοῦλος: "servant" in Jowett, "subject" in Cornford (followed by H. D. P. Lee) in their translations of this passage, are surely too weak for δοῦλος here. That "chattel slave" is *not* meant here is no objection: neither is "slave" in English confined to this more restricted sense which is the

divine thing in him—not that we think the slave should be so ruled to his own hurt, as Thrasymachus thought about the governed, but because it is best for everyone to be ruled by the divine and rational thing—preferably his own and in him, or else imposed on him from the outside, so that so far as possible we may all be alike and friends, governed by the same thing.

Here in microcosm is Plato's vision of just relations between two persons whose luck in the natural lottery has been grossly unequal. The one with low congenital endowment of intelligence ought to be, and for his own good, so stripped of any right to self-determination that Plato (who is not squeamish—he is not Benjamin Jowett) does not hold back from using δοῦλος to describe that role, though well aware that the word is one of the ugliest in the language: few carry stronger charges of scorn and terror. Plato uses it nonetheless, confident that he can upgrade it, purge it of this ugliness by marrying it to one of the most attractive: φίλος. Plato's message is that the δοῦλος can be φίλος. The punch line is "so that so far as possible, we may all be alike and friends, governed by the same thing;" but, the punch is weakened in English because "friend" is not as strong as φίλος.[101] Plato is not speaking of two people who just happen to be on good, friendly terms, exchanging pleasantries at the street corner, and the like. That in itself would be remarkable enough, considering that one of them is said to be the other's "slave." We might have expected that such a surrender of one's freedom to another human being would leave one bitterly resentful, nursing a scarcely concealed hostility for the man who stands over one's head with the right to dictate one's every action. But when Plato speaks of the manual worker as the intellectual's φίλος it is love, not mere friendship, that he means—love according to Plato's

---

*primary* one of δοῦλος and the *exclusive* one of ἀνδράποδον. With the use of δοῦλος here cf. that of δουλεία in 563D6, κἂν ὁτιοῦν δουλείας τις προσφέρηται: here too the word is not meant in its literal sense of chattel slavery, but to make Plato's point the word should still be rendered "slavery" (as it is by Lindsay, as is also δοῦλος in the present passage).

101 Thus, consider Apollo's statement about Admetus in Euripides' *Alcestis* (15), πάντας δ' ἐλέγξας καὶ διεξελθὼν φίλους. How ludicrous it would be to take this to be saying that Admetus made the round of his *friends*, asking each in turn if one of them would die for him. No one in his senses could address such a question to persons other than those to whom one is bound by the deepest ties of love. Needless to say, φίλος is not always used in so strong a sense. But its normal use is stronger enough than that of *friend* to make φίλους exactly right in the above statement, where "friends" would be hopelessly wrong (unless qualified, directly or by the context). And cf. *PS*, 4.

understanding,[102] sustained by solidarity in the pursuit of happiness and excellence, since each gives indispensable support to the other's quest: If they did not have each other, both would fail: the philosopher, for he would then have to divert precious time and energy to meaningless drudgery; the manual worker too would fail, and more disastrously, for without direction from above his life would be bestial: he would be ruled "by the brood of beasts within him." [103] So only by pooling their disparate resources, fixed ineluctably for each by nature, can either of them have the chance to find the best life for himself and make the best that can be made of himself. If the worker has even a glimmering of this truth, how could he resent the deprivation of rights which casts him in the role of slave to "the best man"? How could you fail to respond with love to one who stands by you to share with you day by day his "divine" gift of reason?

Plato is making here two remarkable assumptions: on one hand, the natural depravity of non-intellectual man; on the other, the

---

[102] See *PS*, 13 ff.

[103] It should be emphasized that Plato predicates his *apologia* for this type of symbiotic relation solely on the conviction that it is genuine φιλία, and does *not* also argue for it on the ground that (a higher sort of) *freedom* would also be realized in it. When Versenyi produces such an argument on Plato's behalf (*loc. cit.* in n. 98 above) he fails to make it clear to the reader (perhaps does not realize it himself) that it is totally foreign to Plato's own thought. Plato would certainly agree with Versenyi that "freedom ... is good only to the extent that it is accompanied by knowledge" and that "this is the freedom Plato's state is designed to provide." But Plato would *not* have said that "this (Platonic) state, *far from denying freedom*, liberates man better than any rival polity, be it as 'liberal' as it may" (my emphasis). On the contrary, Plato would recognize that his state *does* deny freedom to most of its citizens (for their own good, of course) and that there is to be far less freedom in his state than in contemporary Athens, which in his view (557B-558B; 562B-564A) is swimming (and drowning) in freedom. That is the whole point of his speaking of the manual worker's relation to the philosopher in our passage as "slavery." When Plato runs up the flag of "freedom," side by side with φιλία and "wisdom," as he does (only) in the *Laws* (693B, 701D; cf. Appendix C below) it is not because he has found his way to a sublimated concept of freedom (such as St. Paul was to epitomize in the phrase, "whose service is perfect freedom"), but because he has *given up* the paradigm of δουλεία of producer to philosopher he had championed with full conviction in the *Republic*, has turned away from political absolutism, and is now arguing for a "mixed constituion," a mean between "monarchy" and "democracy" (697C, 699E, 756E), still presenting δουλεία and freedom as opposites (694A). The δουλεία to which he now gives unqualified approval is *slavery to the laws*—not to a man, no matter how enlightened (700A; and cf. the new conception of state officials as "servants of the laws" ([ὑπηρέτας τοῖς νόμοις, 715C-D]).

intellectual man's capacity for incorruptible virtue. The manual worker, congenitally weak in reason, if granted the right to make autonomous moral choices for himself, would make predictably bad ones, and if he had the power to indulge them, his life would be, like the tyrant's in Book IX, a seething mass of sensuality, cupidity, and vanity. For such a man hope of salvation lies only in living under another's moral tutelage. The intellectual, on the other hand, Plato credits with such marvellous perfectibility that having other human beings completely in his power could not corrupt him. His check over the "brood of beasts" within *him* would be so secure that he would never yield to the temptation to treat his "slave" as anything but a friend.

How was it that Plato found both of these assumptions reasonable? The answer lies in that deeper, meta-normative, stratum of his thought, the metaphysical subsoil of his moral philosophy, his two-world doctrine of reality. This is, of course, well-known; no one could miss it; the central books of the *Republic* are given over to it. But not all of its links with the moral and political doctrine that preceded are on the surface, though they are not far below it either. The one that strikes me as the most significant is this: Plato's bifurcation of reality produces a bifurcation of humanity.[104] It breaks up the human family into two different breeds of men. One, by far the largest, is doomed to live outside the real world of truth and value; it will never know the eternal Forms of Justice, Beauty, Goodness and the rest. The moral judgments of such persons, and not only their judgments—the valuations that govern the longings, anxieties, and terrors of their lives—are either second-hand, consisting of what they have been *told* is just and good and beautiful, or else, when first-hand, are hedonic calculations within the sense-bound world of their experience:[105] their soul, stuck

---

[104] For an analogous (and no less devastating) division of humanity within Aristotle's very different metaphysical framework see J. M. Rist, "Aristotle: The Value of Man and the Origin of Morality," *Canadian Journal of Philosophy* 4 (1974), 1-21.

[105] If one of Plato's cave-dwellers were to venture beyond the moral standards he has been taught by his betters and try to figure out for himself the rights and wrongs of conduct, he would be lost. All he would reach by his own efforts would be the pseudo-morality Plato described in the *Phaedo* as a calculus of hedonic utilities ("exchanging pleasures for pleasures, pains for pains, fears for fears, like coins, the smaller for the bigger, the bigger for the smaller" (69A)) producing the fake virtue of persons who are "temperate because of intemperance" and "brave because of cowardice" (68D-69A)): cf. *PS*, 137, n. 79.

inside an animal, knows only animal pleasures—the ones to pacify
the greedy tastebuds, the itchy epidermis, of the polymorphous
brute. People in this predicament can make no proper estimates of
happiness.[106] Their pains are real enough, but most of what they
know of joy is only relief from pain, illusion of pleasure, a grey
mistaken for white against the black.[107] This is how Plato pictures
their lot:

> Bent over their tables, they batten like cattle with stooping heads and
> eyes glued to the ground; so they guzzle and copulate, and in their
> insatiable greed they kick and butt one another to death with horns
> and hooves of steel, because they can never satisfy with these unreal
> things the part of themselves which is itself unreal and is incapable of
> lasting satisfaction.[108]

Now think of the other breed. When the philosopher breaks out of
the shadow-world of the Cave into the light-filled, sun-drenched,
world of Form, what he achieves is not only intellectual illumination
but, simultaneously, in one and the same experience, moral regen-

---

[106] The far-reaching political implications of the doctrine of false pleasure
in the *Republic* have seldom been noticed. The doctrine seals the disqualifi-
cation of non-philosophers to make judgments concerning the general
happiness; they are not even fit judges of *their own* happiness.

[107] 584E7-585A5:

> And would it surprise you if those who have had no experience of the
> real thing make many unsound judgments, and when it comes to
> pleasure and pain and the in-between state, they are so conditioned
> that when moving into pain their impressions are correct—they really
> are in pain—but, when moving from pain to the in-between state, though
> they do have a strong impression of getting fulfilment and pleasure,
> they are fooled; like men who compare grey only with black, having
> had no experience of white, they are only comparing pain with the lack
> of it, having had no experience of pleasure?

Plato is not suggesting that the illusion he is describing can occur only in
the case he mentions, i.e. when relief from pain is mistaken for pleasure.
In his earlier description (583C ff.) the phenomenon is perfectly symmetrical:
hedonic illusion may occur when loss of pleasure is felt as pain (583E1-2;
584A4-8) as in the converse case. His point in the passage I have cited is
best understood if one recalls his doctrine that, with trivial exceptions
(e.g. that of odours in 584B), the "real" pleasures are intellectual, hence
out of the range of the mass-man's experience. He is the man Plato is
talking about in the citation: he knows the black of the hedonic scale (physical pain is as real for him as for the philosopher) but not its upper ranges of
dazzling white (spiritual bliss is a closed book to him), so he mistakes for
pleasure his moments of relief from pain. This is the pervasive delusion of
his life, endemic to his condition, and Plato is content to disregard the
opposite error because he thinks its incidence would be negligible in this
case.

[108] 586A-B, translation mainly after Cornford.

eration.[109] To see the Form of Justice out there in all its beauty, irradiated by the Good, is not only to recognize in it the truth behind all of his previous gropings after it, but to be seized with a love for it which fills him with passionate longing to make it the ordering principle of his own life and of the life of his πόλις. This is the mystical element at the core of Plato's metaphysics. I call it "mystical" because no fully rational explanation can be given of the implosion set off in the philosopher's soul by the vision of Form which makes a new man out of him. The varieties of mysticism are legion. It can be wholly this-worldly, as in Zen. In Plato it is radically other-worldly—as much so as in Augustine or Paul. Through Plato we get a glimpse of what Christian otherworldliness would have been like if it had not been informed by ἀγάπη and its ethics had not been humanized by the man-centeredness of its Jewish God. A moment ago, speaking for humanistic ethics, I said that when I ask, "What is excellence for?" I can only reply: "For humanity." Plato would protest that my question is senseless: excellence, he would say, eternally complete in the world of Form, is not for anything or anyone: it simply *is*, and its imperative to us is only the imperious love its being evokes in any soul capable of knowing it. He would turn my question around: "What is humanity for?" he would ask. And his reply would not be so unlike the one in the Westminster Confession. Substitute "Form" for "God" and it would be the same: The chief end of man is to glorify Form and enjoy it for ever. If you are a Platonic philosopher, you have found the meaning of your life, your true vocation, in faithful service to the Forms of Justice, Beauty, Goodness, and the rest. You are

---

[109] Cf. the citation from 500C2-D1 in n. 87 above, and cf. the representation of vision of Form in the *Symposium* (212A) as a procreative union which issues in the birth of "real virtue, not images of it," and in the corresponding passage in the *Republic* about the philosopher's "real union with reality" (490B5) from which "a sound and just disposition, accompanied by σωφροσύνη" (490C) is bound to follow. Cf. also the earlier description of the philosopher's "unremitting passion for any knowledge that will reveal to him that reality which is eternal and immune to the vagaries of generation and decay" (485 B1-3), a passion which absorbs most of the psychic energy that in other men usually goes into concupiscence (485D6-12: the "hydraulic" metaphor), so that he becomes "temperate and free from the love of money" (485E3) and could not be "a bad partner (δυσσύμβολος) or unjust" (486B7). I have touched all too briefly on this aspect of Platonic mysticism in *PS*, 52, and regret that I did not pursue it elsewhere in that book, failing to do so in section VI. 2. ii of the essay on "Justice and Happiness in the *Republic*" where it is particularly relevant.

possessed by a transcendent love beside which earthly passions pale. You have discovered bliss which turns the prizes of this world into trash.[110]

I started off in this paper with a semantic investigation and find myself now in the thick of mystical metaphysics. Let me state more clearly than I have yet done the rationale of the itinerary. The gravest charge brought against Plato within my life-time has been the imputation of bad faith: knowing that justice meant equality, Plato made it mean inequality "to make propaganda for his totalitarian state." The quotation is from page 92 of Sir Karl Popper's *Open Society and its Enemies*.[111] Though my object in this paper has not been to defend Plato's theory—as is abundantly clear by now, I consider it indefensible—but only to understand it, I could scarcely have achieved my end without facing up to the charge that the theory had been, to begin with, a well-intentioned [112] lie. Accordingly I dealt at some length with the claim that Plato severs all of the ancient ties of justice with equality. Made plausible in the extreme by the fact that there is not a word about equality in Plato's formulation of the theory, I argued that

---

[110] "Trash" or "nonsense" (φλυαρία) Plato uses repeatedly to underscore the triviality of the sensible and the sensual in contrast to the ideal and intellectual: *Phaedo* 69C, the body "fills us with loves and appetites and fears and all sorts of phantoms and trash"; *Republic* 515D, the philosopher, once out of the Cave, will come to understand that all he saw there was "trash"; *Symposium* 211E, the Idea of Beauty, seen at the height of the ascent, is "beauty unalloyed, pure, unmixed, not full of human flesh and color and a lot of other mortal trash." And Plato has many other images for the trashiness of physical things and satisfactions: they are "images," "phantoms," "shadows": they are "small" (in the *Theaetetus* [173E], he adds "and nothings" [σμικρὰ καὶ οὐδέν]).—It may be asked: If we were to take Plato at his word on this point, should we not have to infer that the philosopher's renunciations of material sources of happiness would cost him nothing? The answer is that so they would, if he were a discarnate soul; in his present state of incarnation he is bound to desire intensely the creature-comforts of property and sex and to feel the cost of their deprivation.

[111] "Why did Plato claim, in the *Republic*, that justice meant inequality if, in general usage, it meant equality? To me the only likely reply seems to be that he wanted to make propaganda for his totalitarian state by persuading the people that it was the 'just' state ... But his attack on equalitarianism was not an honest attack" (92-93).

[112] Popper has never questioned the good intentions of Plato's totalitarianism: "... I believe in the sincerity of Plato's totalitarianism ... his ideal was not the maximum exploitation of the working classes by the upper class; it was the stability of the whole" (108).

it is nonetheless false, for if we look beyond the verbal texture of
the theory to its normative force, we will find that it is firmly
committed to that formal equality which is the backbone of
justice and that it dictates a measure of substantive equality in
one area of the life of the πόλις , the economic. At that point I
had to ask myself how Plato could still be led to wipe out every
vestige of human, as distinct from functional, rights, thereby
stripping his fellow-townsmen not only of those rights that an-
swered to the greatest achievement of their corporate life—partici-
patory democracy—but even of their individual right to moral
autonomy, all this unflinchingly in the cause of impartial justice.
The shock of the encounter with a moral vision so alien to one's
own, so hostile to one's deepest convictions, may shake its credibil-
ity, and the temptation to think it dishonest may then be over-
whelming. That is the point at which I had to turn to its background assumptions, first in moral psychology and ultimately in
metaphysics. These are the ones I have laid out in the terminal
part of this paper. Had I shared them I would not have found
Plato's view of justice incredible. I might have found it compelling.

In matters of intellectual honesty proof of the pudding comes
after the eating, sometimes a long time after. Suppose that in
your middle years you give the world a theory that is so brilliantly
original, so stamped with your individuality, that now for you and
others your ego and the theory are inextricably tangled up. Decades
later it begins to dawn on you that something about that theory
is not quite right—confused or false. What will you do then?
Will you suppress the doubt? Or will you look as hard at the new
evidence which threatens your theory as you once did at the old
which shored it up? If my reading of the *Parmenides* as "record of
honest perplexity" is correct,[113] that is what Plato did when doubts
assailed him about his greatest creation, the Theory of Forms.
And just this, surely, is what he did still later to his theory of
Justice. In this case I think there is no "if" about it.[114] No serious

---

113 "The Third Man Argument in the *Parmenides*", *Philos. Review* 62
(1954), 319-49, (reprinted in R. E. Allen, *Studies in Plato's Metaphysics*
[London, 1965], 231-264) Section D, "The Record of Honest Perplexity."
114 As there decidedly is in the case of the import of the *Parmenides*
where my interpretation, though shared by a number of scholars, is strongly
contested by others: some have seen the *Parmenides* as an outright admission
by Plato that his theory is logically bankrupt and has to be abandoned, while

reader of the *Laws* could reasonably doubt that Plato wrote into it, without the slightest hedging, propositions which contradict the very tenets I have presented in this paper as indispensable supports of his meta-normative theory of justice.[115] He now declares flatly that no mortal nature can bear without corruption the strain of autocratic power (713C; cf. 691C and 875A-D); his former faith—that one who surrenders his power of self-determination to a philosophic master will never have cause to rue it—has now collapsed.[116] And Plato now declares with equal conviction that "slaves and masters can never be friends" (757A); the faith that the δοῦλος can be φίλος has also collapsed.[117]

Seeing this we could guess that the allocation of rights which had left the great majority of the civic body politically disfranchised is now far from anything Plato's sense of justice would approve. We do not need to guess. We see Plato rehabilitating in the *Laws* many of those democratic rights he had wiped out in the *Republic*. Though he does not discuss the earlier theory, does not allude to it

---

others, at the other extreme, have seen there nothing more than a didactic exercise in which Plato warns his public against plausible misinterpretations of his theory.

[115] See Appendix C below.

[116] In a review article which appeared in 1957 (reprinted in *PS*, 204 ff. at 212-216) I discussed this drastic modification in Plato's system of political beliefs, arguing there that the change must have occurred after the composition of the *Politicus*, and conjecturing that it must have come after the third journey to Syracuse which dashed for good whatever hopes he had still cherished that under suitable instruction Dionysius the Younger might yet become a philosopher king.

[117] The sentence I have quoted is no mere *obiter dictum*. It articulates a doctrine which Plato expresses with fervor, if not with full consistency, in the *Laws*. He introduces it in Book III, where he announces the new-found trinity of political norms: "the πόλις should be free, intelligent, and in amity with itself (ἐλευθέραν τε ... καὶ ἔμφρονα καὶ ἑαυτῇ φίλην)," 693B; (cf. 701D and n. 103 above). He proceeds to explain the bond he now sees between φιλία and freedom: "Monarchy" and "democracy" (representing, respectively, extremes of "slavery" and "freedom" (694A) are the political archetypes ("mother"-forms); constitutions "must of necessity partake of both, if there is to be freedom and φιλία along with wisdom" (693D-E). He reinforces this with a pseudo-historical moralistic homily in which the Persians flourish under an idealized Cyrus because under him "they maintained the due mean (τὸ μέτριον) between slavery and freedom ... For when rulers gave subjects a share of freedom (ἐλευθερίας ... μεταδιδόντες) and advanced them towards equality (ἐπὶ τὸ ἴσον ἄγοντες) the soldiers were more φίλοι with their officers," etc.; "consequently at that time they made progress in every way because of freedom, φιλία, and shared intelligence" (694A-B).

in any way, we can be certain he has abandoned it.[118] I do not know of any other case where the creator of a major philosophical theory moved out of it so coolly when he found himself unable to give continuing adherence to its supporting assumptions.[119]

### APPENDIX A

In view of the repeated criticisms I have been making in this paper of *The Open Society and its Enemies*, I beg to explain two things:

(1) My strictures are offered in a spirit of high respect for its author's stature as a philosopher, and also for his courageous counter-affirmation of great liberal principles whose denial by Plato has been all too often soft-pedalled—at times even justified—by scholars. In its *confessio fidei* I find *The Open Society and its Enemies* entirely admirable. My disagreements with its treatment of Plato are solely over questions of scholarly interpretation which are matters of legitimate and indeed unavoidable argument: when one's conclusions are at variance with those of an influential author, to shirk controversy would scarcely betoken esteem for him or for his subject.

(2) My criticisms would have been unnecessary if in the course of the three decades that have elapsed since its publication its gravest misunderstandings of Plato's theory of justice had either been corrected (even in part) by Popper himself or else had been nailed down by his numerous critics. Neither of these things has happened. In the "Addenda" to the 1962 edition of his book Popper says he "changed [his] mind on Plato's physical cosmology between the first and second editions" of the book, but not on Plato's moral and political philosophy (335). Nor have the errors in the

---

[118] In the *Laws* we see neither hide nor hair of the "doing one's own" definiens of δικαιοσύνη. What then, exactly, is the theory of social justice that Plato has settled for in the *Laws*? The answer is not clear. Earlier (n. 83) I referred to his (apparently) total endorsement of "proportional equality": to call this ἀληθεστάτην καὶ ἀρίστην ἰσότητα (757B6), to say that it is Διὸς κρίσις (B7) and that τὸ πρέπον . . . ἀπονέμει (C5-6) and, finally, that τὸ πολιτικόν ("true policy") lies in following out "precisely *this* justice" (τοῦτ' αὐτὸ τὸ δίκαιον, C6-7) is, on the face of it, to recognize proportional equality as the very essence of justice. However, immediately after saying this, Plato proceeds to concede that the "arithmetical equality" of the lot ("the equality of measure and weight and number" (757B6-7)), which is "virtually opposite (to proportional equality) in its practical import" (757B2-3), must *also* be employed, though only as a matter of practical necessity (ἀναγκαῖον, 757D5; ἀνάγκη, E3)—without it civic discord would ensue (757D7-E1)—and used "as little as possible" (ὅτι μάλιστα ἐπ' ὀλίγοις, 758A1). Whatever may be the upshot of this curious compromise between "the two equalities" (a big dose of one of them, with a dash of the other), it should be evident that the end result is a far cry from the theory of distributive justice in the *Republic*, since that theory (i) is by no means committed to "proportional equality," as I have argued in Section II, and (ii) does not need to be compromised by its opposite for the sake of avoiding civic discord, for it is conceived as being itself the very means of fostering civic φιλία (as I have argued in Section III).

[119] See Appendix C below.

latter area been fully identified and rebutted by other scholars. Even the best of the original reviews known to me—Richard Robinson's, "Dr. Popper's Defense of Democracy," *Philos. Rev.* 60 (1951), 487-507—conceded too much. Thus Robinson appears to agree with Popper that Plato "aimed at the good of a superbeing, 'the city as a whole', rather than at the goods [*sic*] of all the citizens" (493). And when protesting the claim that Plato's silence on equality as a basic ingredient of justice was dishonestly manipulative, Robinson tacitly concedes it, affirming only (what Popper never denied: see n. 112 above) that it was well-intentioned ("If Plato deliberately kept quiet about the equalitarian view of justice, he did so with good intentions towards men . . ." [500]). The most comprehensive critique, R. B. Levinson, *In Defense of Plato* (Cambridge, Mass., 1953), a work of earnest and industrious scholarship, succeeds in throwing much light on disputed passages and repeatedly supplies a useful corrective to one-sided claims in Popper, but fails as a defense of Plato because it misses the very substantial measure of truth in some of Popper's charges (beginning with the charge of "totalitarianism") while, conversely, it appears to concede a claim of Popper's— that "only the members of the ruling class are educated" (267, n. 13)— which should most certainly have been challenged, for it is a mainstay of the brutal ("human cattle") view of the lower classes Popper ascribes to Plato; and there is not a particle of direct evidence for it (see the best Popper can do for it: 227, n. 33, and 267, n. 13), while there is a strong (in my opinion, conclusive) case against it (for the lines along which it may be made see *PS*, 137, and my rebuttal of Guthrie's sponsorship of the same view in Vol. 4 of his *History of Greek Philosophy* [Cambridge, 1975] in my review of the book in the *Times Literary Supplement* for Dec. 12, 1975, 1474-75).

## APPENDIX B
### (for note 96)

The concept of a human being as "an end in himself", introduced by Kant, needs to be freed from a grave defect in his formulation of it, as I have pointed out briefly in "Justice and Equality" (cited in n. 11 above, 48-49). I referred to that discussion of Kant's phrase in *PS*, 10, n. 24 (the reference is indispensable for my use of the phrase in my essay on "The Individual as an Object of Love in Plato"), and I hope to expand that discussion in a sequel to the present essay. For the present the following may suffice: I accept without reservation Kant's basic distinction between *things*, whose value is *conditional* (it depends on their being valued by someone, p. 57 of the Rosen-kranz-and-Shubert edition of the *Grundlegung der Metaphysik der Sitten*) and *replaceable* (whatever has this kind of value "can be replaced by something else which is equivalent," *op. cit.*, 65) and which we may use as mere means to our own ends, and, on the other hand, *persons*, whose value (or "dignity," *Würde*) being *unconditional* and *irreplaceable*, we may never so use. When he proceeds to identify implicitly the latter sort of value with *moral merit* (see the quotation in note 40 of "Justice and Equality"), I dissent. This is surely an error, and its consequences would be disastrous: the identification would entail that a person's moral achievement is the only thing which endows him with unconditional and irreplaceable value and interdicts use of him by others as mere means to their ends. Were this true, a person's value would not be unconditional, for *it would be forfeited in case of moral failure*, and this is surely false: moral failure may call for censure and punishment, but these are themselves predicated on the assumption that a delinquent remains a person and retains the special value which attaches to persons in contradistinction to things, as Kant himself would be the first to recognize. Once the Kantian conception has been purged of this error, we are left with the notion of a person who as an end-in-himself has value for himself, valuing his own existence and all other persons and things from his own unique subjective point of view, and does not need to be valued by anyone else in order to have that kind of value ("the value of the valuer," as I speak of it in "Justice and Equality," *loc. cit.*). In respect of this kind of value, which all men share with one another and with no other creature in the physical universe, all men are of equal value.

## APPENDIX C
### (for notes 115 and 119)

Paul Shorey, fervent apostle of the "unity of Plato's thought," pushed it so far as to maintain that even the *Laws* marked no substantial change in Plato's doctrines ("Plato's 'Laws' and the Unity of Plato's Thought," *Classical Philology* 9 (1914), 345-369). It is instructive to see what happens when he seeks to maintain his thesis in the face of those two drastic changes to which I have referred in the text above and in the three preceding notes:

(1) The statement that "slaves and masters can never be friends" (757A1), which contradicts so flatly the doctrine of *Republic* 590C-D, is simply ignored. So are the thrice-repeated assertions (693B3-4, 693D8-E1, 701D7-9) enunciating the new trinity of political goals, where φιλία and ἐλευθερία appear side by side (n. 117 above). I have ransacked the text of Shorey's paper and the many scores of references in its notes without finding a single reference (or even a single allusion) to any of those four passages in the *Laws*. (It should go without saying that the omissions are not due to ignorance—Shorey's knowledge of the Platonic corpus is matchless—nor yet due to the wish to divert the reader's mind from unsettling evidence. We are faced here with the sad spectacle of a very great scholar so blinkered by his preconceptions that he fails to notice all too familiar texts which contradict his theory.)

(2) The passages I cited in the text above in which Plato now records his conviction that autocratic government will corrupt the autocrat are duly recognized in Shorey's paper: he includes references to 691C and 713C and to a part of 875A-D within a string of references in n. 8 to p. 355 in support of the (perfectly correct) statement that in the *Laws* Plato (a) invokes the notion "of a converted autocrat to bring about the revolution and inaugurate reform" but (b) recognizes the impracticability of "benevolent autocracy as a continuing form of government" (355). In the note Shorey calls attention to the fact that *with respect to* (a) there is scarcely any difference in doctrine between the *Laws*, on one hand, and the *Republic* and *Politicus*, on the other. But he blandly ignores the fact that *there is a vast difference with respect to* (b): what is the rule of the philosophers in the *Republic* and of the philosopher-scientist in the *Politicus*, if not "benevolent autocracy as a continuing form of government"? Plato, though well aware of the precariousness of such a form of government, does not say in either of these two dialogues that it is incapable of durable instantiation; in particular, he does not say in either of them, as he does thrice over in the *Laws*, that it is impracticable because the uncorrupted tenure of dictatorial power is beyond human capacity. Later (358) Shorey remarks (I intersperse reference-marks in the quotation) that "the paradoxical communism of the *Republic* is (i)

Library of
Davidson College

mainly designed to impose disinterestedness on the guardians, and (ii) thus in a measure anticipates the objection of the *Laws* and *Politicus* that human nature cannot endure unlimited power." Shorey is, of course, correct in the case of (i). But in the case of (ii) he ignores the vital difference that in the *Republic* Plato lays down institutional arrangements which he believes *can* enable the human nature of his philosophers to bear unlimited power without corruption, but undertakes no such thing in the *Laws*, for the very good reason that he has now come to believe that this weakness in human nature is incurable. (For Shorey's assimilation of the position of the *Politicus* to that of the *Laws* in the preceding quotation cf n. 116 above.)

## ADDITIONAL NOTE

The principal translations of the *Republic* to which I have referred (by name of author only) in this paper are as follows:

Bloom, A. (New York, 1968).
Cornford, F. M. (New York, 1945).
Jowett, B., 3rd ed. (Oxford, 1892); 4th ed., revised by D. J. Allan and H. E. Dale (Oxford, 1953).
Lindsay, A. D. (London, 1906).
Robin, L. (Paris, 1950).
Schleiermacher, Fr., revised by Kurz, D. (Darmstadt, 1971).
Shorey, P. (London, 1930).

# PLATO ON LAW AND NATURE

## MARTIN OSTWALD

It is a reasonable assumption that the birth of Plato in 427 B.C. created less of a stir among the Athenian intelligentsia than did the arrival of Gorgias, famous as an orator and teacher of rhetoric, at the head of an embassy from Leontini,[1] for the arrival of any renowned intellectual in the "capital of wisdom of Greece," as some called Athens,[2] always created a stir. Seven years earlier, if we can trust Plato's dates, Protagoras' presence had caused a similar excitement.[3] The young intellectuals crowded into the house of his host Callias to meet and learn from this professional educator [4] that expertise in politics which he claimed to be able to impart.[5] On other occasions, they will have sat at the feet of philosophers such as Anaxagoras, Democritus, and Archelaus, who had made the study of nature (φύσις) their special province, perpetuating a pursuit that had begun with Thales a century and a half earlier in far-away Ionia.[6] The intellectual atmosphere generated by these men produced in the last quarter of the fifth century a lively debate on whether law or nature does or should determine the views, acts, and social behavior of men. "Law" and "nature" do not render quite accurately their Greek equivalents νόμος and φύσις. Νόμος is, by and large, anything determined and regarded as valid by men; it includes human customs, conventions, and beliefs as well as the political institutions and legal enactments under which men live. The term φύσις on the other hand, describes the way things are and the way they work, immutably, eternally, of necessity, neither initiated nor changeable by human action, and independent of human thought.

---

[1] Diodorus 12.53.2, cf. Thucydides 3.86.3.

[2] Plato, *Protagoras* 337D5-6.

[3] Ib. 309 C13-311A7, 314E3-315B8; for 433 B.C. as the probable dramatic date of the *Protagoras*, see W. K. C. Guthrie, *A history of Greek philosophy* 3 (Cambridge, 1969) 263 with n. 5.

[4] Plato, *Protagoras* 317B4-5.

[5] Ib. 319A4: τὴν πολιτικὴν τέχνην.

[6] For the presence of these philosophers in Athens at this time, see Guthrie, *op. cit.* 2 (Cambridge, 1965) 347-9.

The debate on the priority of νόμος or of φύσις began in Athens about the time Plato was born, and it remained an issue throughout the fourth century and even beyond. In a sense, the issue is alive today: the attacks upon the Establishment in the late sixties in the name of "legitimacy" may be regarded as an attack upon νόμος under the banner of principles of social justice which derive their content ultimately from some view of φύσις; similarly, the feminist movement is poised against νόμοι, which, as its proponents claim, fail to do justice to what φύσις has given to women. Neither Plato nor, it seems, Socrates found it necessary to take a stand on the side of either νόμος or φύσις in this debate. But the debate itself was an important point of departure, and its resolution the final result, of Plato's political philosophy. From Socrates Plato had learned that there can be no excellence in private or in public life without knowledge: without knowledge of what is right under all circumstances one cannot act rightly nor be a righteous person. By confronting the issues raised in the νόμος-φύσις debate, Plato developed the Socratic maxim in two directions. He showed, first, as I shall argue, that the teaching of the rhetoricians and sophists, having adapted to its own ends the doctrines of the natural philosophers, had led to the perversion of Athenian politics. The second and more positive direction was to identify the objects of moral knowledge and to base upon them a science of society and politics which would bring authentic social justice to mankind.

Plato's criticism of the effects of the teaching of the sophists and rhetoricians on Athenian politics faces different aspects of the νόμος-φύσις debate in the *Gorgias* and in the *Protagoras*. The *Gorgias* confronts the political activists in the person of Callicles, a pupil of the great rhetorician after whom the dialogue is named. There is no doubt in Callicles' mind that the true standard of justice is set by nature. But what he means by "nature" is shown to be narrow, negative, and nihilistic: nature, Callicles claims, makes us seek to gratify our desires to the full, regardless of its consequences to others.[7] The capacity for full gratification is given only to a few men and their superior power makes it right that they should have dominion over the weak:[8] this is, in Callicles' paradoxical expression, "the law of nature," the νόμος τῆς φύσεως, the only true

---

[7] Plato, *Gorgias* 491E6-492A3.
[8] Ib. 483C6-D6.

law.[9] What is commonly called "law" is in fact a set of unnatural arbitrary rules [10] which the weak enact and falsely call "just" in order to protect themselves against what is truly just, namely the claim of the superior power of the strong.[11] Tyranny and despotism are the ultimate aims of the strong; to attain them they can and must trample upon the laws of the weak.[12]

Socrates' refutation involves a complete revaluation of both φύσις and νόμος in the light of his conviction that it takes a certain skill or expertise—the Greek term is τέχνη—to live a good life.[13] Callicles had made himself vulnerable by saying that the strong need intelligence and courage to fulfil their desires.[14] But, as Socrates points out, it takes no intelligence but only a knack to indulge in pleasures; but to differentiate good from harmful pleasures, or, as he puts it, to find the "nature and true source" of pleasure, requires intelligence and expert skill (τέχνη).[15] Callicles' view of φύσις has thus been undermined: true intelligence is not part of a nature that sanctions the use of brute force, but it investigates the nature which constitutes the true reality of a given phenomenon, in this case pleasure. Another instance of τέχνη is brought in to demonstrate the perverted view Callicles takes of political activism: a physician—so often in Plato the example of an expert *par excellence*—practises his skill not in order to get for himself more food and drink than anyone else [16] but to introduce regularity and order into the body that lacks it, and he does so on the basis of knowledge of what constitutes a healthy body. Similarly, a true orator will not, as Callicles is compelled to do, flatter the masses in order to realise his political ambitions, but he will know and foster in the souls of his audience that regularity and order which, in Socrates' words, is tantamount to justice and self-control.[17] Law has thus been transformed from the notion of defensive enactments of the weak into a positive norm proper and appropriate to public and private conduct. But what has been

---

[9] Ib. 483E3.
[10] Ib. 492C7.
[11] Ib. 483B4-C6.
[12] Ib. 484A2-C3, 492B1-C8.
[13] Ib. 500A7-C8.
[14] Ib. 492A1-2.
[15] Ib. 495E2-500A6, 501A5-6.
[16] Ib. 490B1-491A6.
[17] Ib. 504D3.

shown, above all, is that Callicles' view of νόμος and φύσις is not
based on the intelligence he claims for it. Intelligence works only
through an expert skill which is based on knowledge and not on
desire.

The confrontation takes a different turn in the *Protagoras*. Its
central figure is not a political activist but a respected professional
educator, who actually claims to possess and to teach πολιτικὴ
τέχνη (or expert skill in politics),[18] which the *Gorgias* had implicitly
established as a desideratum. But, as the dialogue shows, Protagoras cannot deliver what he promises. He credits nature with
having endowed each individual from birth with different talents
so as to enable each of them to excel in a different τέχνη. Only one
skill and the excellence that goes with it comes to men after birth,
and that is political excellence which consists in justice and mutual
respect.[19] Its purpose is to make life in society possible,[20] and for
that reason it is, contrary to all other skills, evenly distributed
among all men. For that reason, too, men attribute its presence not
to nature but to teaching and practice.[21] This view has interesting
consequences: if political excellence belongs to all men alike, and
if it is acquired by teaching and practice, everyone must not only
have it but also be able to impart it; this, in turn, would mean
that its teaching is not the province of specialists but is absorbed
throughout the whole process of growing into an adult. Here
Protagoras' view of νόμος comes in: men learn what is right and
wrong, good and bad, pious and impious [22] first at home, then at
school, and finally "the state in its turn makes them learn the laws
and live after the model which they furnish." [23]

Taken by itself, this position is not too far removed from Socrates'
view in the *Gorgias*, that law is the regularity and order which the
skill of the good orator will create in the soul. But no special skill
is involved here, and Protagoras is, in fact, put in the awkward
position of professing to teach virtue through his expert skill,
while at the same time his belief that moral excellence is taught by
all compels him to deny his own teaching the status of an expert

---

[18] Plato, *Protagoras* 317B4-5, 319A4.
[19] Ib. 322C1-323A7: αἰδὼς καὶ δίκη.
[20] Ib. 323A3.
[21] Ib. 323C5-7: ὅτι δὲ αὐτὴν οὐ φύσει ἡγοῦνται εἶναι οὐδ' ἀπὸ τοῦ αὐτομάτου,
ἀλλὰ διδακτόν τε καὶ ἐξ ἐπιμελείας παραγίγνεσθαι ᾧ ἂν παραγίγνηται.
[22] Ib. 325D3-4.
[23] Ib. 326C7-8.

skill. Protagoras has talked himself out of a job, and the question whether moral excellence can or cannot be taught remains open.

The insight gained in the *Gorgias* and the *Protagoras*, that neither political activists nor the sophists have shown themselves capable of communicating in action or in speech what moral excellence is,[24] made Plato embark on the second and major task which, he felt, the Socratic predication of moral excellence upon knowledge had imposed on him: the identification of the objects on which the skill of living a good life is based and the establishment of a social science on its basis. This quest, which took Plato the rest of his life and which involves the question whether and to what extent law and nature rest on knowable principles, capable of being incorporated into a true social science, will henceforth demand our attention.

The *Meno* lays the foundation for this enterprise in that it demonstrates that objects of knowledge are found through the process of recollection (ἀνάμνησις). In response to Meno's question how one can hope for a definition of virtue without knowing what it is, and how one can be sure of this knowledge once it has been found,[25] Socrates offers a startling proof that all learning is nothing but recollection of knowledge gained by the soul before its incarnation in a body. Through question and answer he elicits from Meno's untutored slave the correct solution of the problem of doubling the area of a given square. From this procedure he concludes that, since the slave had never been faced with this problem before yet is able to follow the demonstration given by Socrates at every step, there must be in him something acquired before his birth that enables him to recognise as truths what is being presented to him. This "something" is a knowledge absorbed by the soul before its incarnation, which question and answer has enabled it to recollect.[26] In this particular case, the knowledge recollected involves immutable and absolute mathematical facts; but Socrates claims that the same procedure can retrieve also knowledge "concerning virtue and other matters" on the ground that all nature is akin, so that recollection of one thing will lead to the discovery of everything else.[27] The possibility of knowledge thus presupposes

---

[24] Plato, *Meno* 93E10-94E2, 95B9-96D4.
[25] Ib. 80D5-8.
[26] Ib. 86A7-B5.
[27] Ib. 81C9-D4.

a new view of nature in which all things are akin. This view will
not be elaborated until the *Timaeus* and the *Laws*; but we recognise
already that the objects of knowledge belong to an invisible realm,
accessible only through the soul, which must have had an independent existence before it came to be housed in our body.

What specifically are some of the objects of mathematical and
moral knowledge we learn in the *Phaedo*, where knowledge as
recollection becomes a cornerstone in the proof of the immortality
of the soul. In order to explain our ability to make true judgments
on what is just, beautiful, good, pious, equal, big, and small,
Plato posits the existence of invisible absolute standards apart
from and independent of the things we experience through our
senses.[28] We gain knowledge of these immutable and eternal
entities only through recollection of what our soul experienced
before its incarnation in the body. Without this knowledge we
cannot correctly discriminate between what is small or large,
equal or unequal, just, beautiful, good, and pious in the many
particular objects and actions in this world. In order to be knowable,
an object must have being, that is, it must not merely exist but
exist without change and for all time. This is not the case with the
world in which we live: here nothing is permanent, things constantly
come into being, change, and pass away again. It is the world of
Becoming, not of Being, and to the extent that anything in it is
knowable it depends on its participation in the absolutes. In
other words, only the presence of absolutes enables us to make
true judgments that something we experience is equal, good, just,
and so forth.[29] These absolutes, which are Plato's most revolutionary
contribution to philosophy, are usually referred to as "Forms,"
because Plato uses the Greek equivalents, εἶδος and ἰδέα, more
frequently than any other expressions to describe them. However,
"Form" never becomes a technical term in Plato. In many cases
a number of different expressions, including "the just itself,"
"the good itself in its own terms," etc. are used to differentiate
the absolutes, accessible to thought alone, from the many just,
good, equal, etc. things which we perceive through our senses.

---

[28] Plato, *Phaedo* 65D4-66A10 (just, beautiful, good); 75D1 (pious);
74A9-75C6, 78D3 (equal); 75C9, 100B6, E5-6 (big and small). For the just,
see also 75D1; for the beautiful 75C11, 76D8, 77A4, 78D3, 100B6 and C3-7;
for the good 75D1, 76D8, 77A4, and 100B6.

[29] Ib. 72E3-75D6, 99D4-105E7.

The science of society and of politics which is established in the *Republic* not only is based on knowledge of the Forms but also relates that knowledge and the τέχνη through which it can be implemented in a novel way to φύσις. A new statement on the nature of νόμος and φύσις forms the point of departure. Thrasymachus presents a thesis of νόμος which combines features of the views with which we are familiar from Callicles and from Protagoras. His view that the just is what is in the interest of the superior [30] sounds like Callicles. But while Callicles had identified this as a standard of justice (δίκαιον) derived from nature and opposed to the laws enacted by the weak for their protection, Thrasymachus does not appeal to φύσις, but sees an expression of what is just in the laws which the rulers enact to secure whatever is to their advantage.[31] This brings him close to the relativism of Protagoras, for whom our notions of right and wrong depend on the laws of the state in which we live. The main difference is that Thrasymachus has the rulers set the standard of justice in enacting their laws: as forms of government differ from state to state, so will the standards of justice embodied in their laws. As Callicles was refuted in the *Gorgias* by an appeal to knowledge and expert skill, so is Thrasymachus in the *Republic*. Socrates points out that, in the first place, a ruler must have knowledge of what is and what is not truly to his advantage; and secondly, that ruling is an expert skill which is practised—again like the skill of a doctor—for the good of those to whom it is applied, not for the benefit of its practitioner. As a doctor's skill improves patients rather than doctors, so a ruler's knowledge is geared to the improvement of his subjects and not to his own profit.[32] So much for Thrasymachus' argument from νόμος.

The arguments from φύσις, which Glaucon advances as a devil's advocate, are less easily settled. Not only rulers but all men, he argues, are naturally [33] out for their own profit. If a sure way of escaping detection were to be found, a man who passes as just would be no less out to get for himself whatever he can than an unjust man. Laws and compacts [34] originated, on this theory, from the need to neutralise the deleterious effects of mutual

---

30 Plato, *Republic* I. 338C1-2.
31 Ib. 1.338E1-339A4.
32 Ib. 1.340D1-342E11.
33 Ib. 2.358E3: πεφυκέναι.
34 Ib. 2.359A3: νόμους καὶ συνθήκας.

aggressiveness, and justice is simply a compromise between doing
wrong with impunity and the inability to get redress for a wrong
sustained. Law is thus not, as it had been for Thrasymachus, the
instrument by which the ruling element enforces its interest, but a
compromise to prevent the destructive instincts of φύσις from
annihilating the human race.

To answer this argument, the rest of the *Republic* is devoted to
the construction in discourse of the scientifically governed society.
By calling it a "state founded in accordance with nature," [35]
Plato tacitly challenges the view of φύσις presupposed by Glaucon.
The scientific state will be based not only on a broader and less
one-sided view of human nature, but also the absolutes on the basis
of which it will be governed are anchored in φύσις. It is to these two
aspects of the *Republic* that we shall now turn.

As far as the human aspect of nature is concerned, the structure
of the state is predicated on the view that nature has endowed
different individuals with different capabilities, and that each
person must perform only that function for which he is fitted by
nature.[36] On the basis of these natural differences, Plato divides
the state into the three classes of Guardians, Auxiliaries, and
Craftsmen, as the social counterpart to the tripartite division of the
soul into a rational, a spirited, and an appetitive element. The
φύσις of each class determines the way in which each shares in the
happiness of the state as a whole.[37] By reason of their philosophic
nature the Guardians rule, and the aim of their training is to
integrate with it the spirited element of their nature, which is the
natural ally of the philosophical.[38] It will be of interest to note here
that Plato regards women as being equally qualified by nature to
become Guardians: they have less physical strength than men do,
but their nature does not differ from the male in any essential
way as far as capacity to rule is concerned.[39]

More immediately important for the implementation of the
"state founded in accordance with nature" is the φιλόσοφος φύσις.
It is characterised by love of learning which reveals the changeless
and eternal entities that are not subject to birth and destruction; [40]

---

[35] Ib. 4.428E7-429A3: κατὰ φύσιν οἰκισθεῖσα πόλις.
[36] Ib. 2.370A7-C5.
[37] Ib. 4.421B3-C6.
[38] Ib. 3.410B5-411C2; cf. 4.441A1-3.
[39] Ib. 5.452E4-456D1, 466D1-4.
[40] Ib. 6.485A10-B3.

it loves truth and hates falsehood,[41] and it tries to grasp the whole of things divine and human.[42] It is disciplined, learns easily, has a retentive memory and a balanced and graceful way of thinking, which will instinctively guide it toward the true Form of each real entity.[43] But these rare and extraordinary qualities carry within them the seeds of their corruption; the masses, drawn by the charismatic brilliance of such men will, by their adulation and promise of worldly success, seduce the philosophic nature into an activist life, which will end up catering to the mob.[44] Education is the only preventative against this kind of corruption,[45] because it brings the philosopher close to that true, changeless and absolute Being for which his natural inclination makes him strive.[46]

We can now turn to the second kind of φύσις which Plato brings in in response to Glaucon. The education of the philosopher culminates in dialectic, the science of rational discussion; all other disciplines merely test whether the student possesses a dialectical nature.[47] In dialectic, "the disparate studies to which they were exposed in the course of their education as children are to be brought together in a comprehensive view of the interrelation of these studies with one another and with the nature of true Being." [48] The philosopher will not rest "until he has attained each essential part of nature with that part of his soul which is fitted to attain such a thing, and the fitting part is the kindred part." [49] We have explicit here what was implied in the *Meno*: there is a kinship in nature between the human mind and the absolutes, and that kinship makes the incarnated soul in the visible world reach out for the invisible. Yet knowledge of the absolutes is not enough. As Plato shows so graphically in the allegory of the Cave,[50] the philosopher must, however reluctantly, return to establish, in the

---

41 Ib. 6.485C3-4, C10-D1.
42 Ib. 6.486A4-6.
43 Ib. 6.486B6-D11.
44 Ib. 6.490C2-492D3.
45 Ib. 6.491D1-492B3.
46 Ib. 6.490A8: πρὸς τὸ ὂν πεφυκὼς εἴη ἁμιλλᾶσθαι.
47 Ib. 7.537C6: μεγίστη. . .πεῖρα διαλεκτικῆς φύσεως.
48 Ib. 7.537C1-3: τά τε χύδην μαθήματα παισὶν ἐν τῇ παιδείᾳ γενόμενα τούτοις συνακτέον εἰς σύνοψιν οἰκειότητός τε ἀλλήλων τῶν μαθημάτων καὶ τῆς τοῦ ὄντος φύσεως.
49 Ib. 6.490B2-4: . . .πρὶν αὐτοῦ ὃ ἔστιν ἑκάστου τῆς φύσεως ἅψασθαι ᾧ προσήκει ψυχῆς ἐφάπτεσθαι τοῦ τοιούτου—προσήκει δὲ συγγενεῖ. . . .
50 Ib. 7.519C8-520A4.

light of his knowledge, a society in which each nature is assigned
its proper place and a government based on eternally and immutably true principles of nature. Since the implementation of the
"state in accordance with nature"—the nature of the philosopher
as its instrument and the nature of true Being as its principles—
will be left to the living rule of the philosopher, there is little
room for νόμος in the *Republic*. The only lawgivers are Socrates
and his interlocutors,[51] and νόμος refers almost exclusively to the
rules and institutions they lay down for the state founded in
accordance with nature.[52]

We have discussed the *Republic* as Plato's major attempt to
establish, in response to political and moral issues raised by the
νόμος-φύσις controversy, a science of politics and society without
which, he claims, "there is no cessation of evils for states, nor, it
seems to me, for mankind." [53] It is a science, complete with a
metaphysical ontology, an epistemology, and a psychology, because
it is founded on absolutes which alone are knowable, since, unlike
the objects of our world of Becoming, they are changeless and
eternal. In the face of this science any conflict between law and
nature vanishes. It is true that the *Republic* remains Plato's major
statement of that science; but, as he came to realise himself, it is
incomplete in that its focus is the rulers, their training, and the
objects of their knowledge. More practical questions about the
manner in which the τέχνη of ruling over less philosophical natures
is to be exercised are hardly, if at all, touched upon. The need to
deal with these questions will have forced itself on Plato partly
as a result of his disappointing experiences as the tutor of Dionysius
II of Syracuse in 366/65 B.C. These experiences will also have
deepened his awareness of the weakness of human nature, of which
a trace first appears in the recognition in the *Republic* that the
philosophic nature can be corrupted. It is a recognition which
makes it questionable whether a true philosopher will ever attain
power, and at the same time emphasises that scientific rule has to
take account of the frailty of those over whom it is to be exercised.

---

[51] Ib. 3.403B4, 417B9; 4.427A4, B1, 429C2; 5.458C6, 462A4; cf. 459E5
and 463C9.

[52] Ib. 2.380C4 and 7, 383C7; 3.415E1; 4.421A5, 425E4, 429C7, 430A2;
5.452C5, 453D2-3, 457B8, C7, 458C3, 461B4, E2, 462A5, 463D2, 465A1, B5,
468B12, and 471B9. The νόμοι of conventional states are rejected or dis-
paraged at 4.427A2 with 425B7-426E8.

[53] Ib. 5.473D5-6.

Accordingly, Plato turned his attention to these practical matters after his return from Syracuse, especially in the *Statesman* and the *Laws* which include new ideas on the function of law in the science of government. But these practical problems are also part of a more general concern with the question of the interaction between the intelligible realm of Being, accessible only to mind, and the world of Becoming in which we live and which we interpret, relying on what we apprehend through our senses. To put it differently, Plato became increasingly concerned with the possibility of gaining knowledge of our world: can we come to know it at all—and, if so, to what extent—if only that which has true Being eternally and immutably can be known as true?

The present framework does not permit me to discuss satisfactorily even those problems alone that are essential for a correct understanding of the relation between nature and law in the later dialogues. I will have to confine myself to what I regard as indispensable, asking the indulgence of those who will have no trouble in detecting how much has been omitted and apologising to those who will find what must be said rather dull and technical. To understand Plato's resolution of the νόμος-φύσις conflict in the tenth book of the *Laws* the problem of the interaction of the invisible world of Being with our visible world of Becoming has to be divided into the following three questions: (1) What is the nature of the universe and of our world?; (2) What is the nature of man and his place in the scheme of things?; and (3) How can, in the light of all this, a human society be instituted in which the principles of scientific government, based on knowledge of the Forms, are realisable?

An incidental discussion of the art of image-making in the *Sophist* lays the foundation for the answer to the question on the nature of the universe and of our world in the *Timaeus*. An image (εἴδωλον), we learn in the *Sophist*, may either be a true copy of an original model (παράδειγμα) or a mere semblance of it.[54] Moreover, when the gods practise the art of image-making, its products are "copies of real things"[55] and consist in "ourselves, all living creatures, and the natural elements of which they are made: fire and water and their kindred."[56] This divine image-maker becomes in

---

[54] Plato, *Sophist* 235B8-236C7.
[55] Ib. 264D4.
[56] Ib. 266B2-3.

the *Timaeus* a divine Demiurge (craftsman), who creates our visible world as a copy upon the model of the unchanging world of Being which includes the Forms.[57] The Model is a Living Being whose nature is eternal;[58] it is called ἡ τοῦ παντὸς φύσις, "the nature of the universe,"[59] "of which all other living beings, individually and in their kinds, are parts," and which "holds and encompasses within itself all intelligible beings."[60] In other words, our world is the copy of an original which is invisible and eternal; it is no less than the nature of everything that is, but as such it and its parts are accessible only to our minds. The divine Demiurge, "wishing to make (our world) most like the intelligible original, most beautiful and perfect in every respect, composed it as one visible animate being, containing within it all living things which are by nature akin to their originals."[61] We have here the beginning of an explanation of the kinship of all nature, of which we first heard in the *Meno*.[62]

As in the *Meno*, the kinship of all nature as well as our ability to gain knowledge of the unseen is attributed to soul, which animates, in Plato's view, not only the world of humans, animals, and vegetables,[63] but also the visible deities of sun, moon, and stars, and the invisible conventional gods. To understand its composition, we have to turn again to an argument in the *Sophist*, which sheds some light on the relation of a copy to its original. Since a true copy, it is argued there, *is* not reality, it cannot have that true Being which can be predicated only of the Forms;[64] nevertheless, inasmuch as it is an accurate copy of true Being, it "exists somehow"[65] as an "intertwining of Being and Non-Being."[66] To explain what can and what cannot be known about the copy, Plato introduces in the *Sophist* the Forms of Sameness (τὸ αὐτόν) and of Difference (τὸ θάτερον), both of which are contained in the Form of Being and, like Being, pervade all other Forms.[67] The

[57] Plato, *Timaeus* 28A6-B1.

[58] Ib. 37D3: αἰώνιος; 38B8 and 39E2: διαιωνία.

[59] Ib. 41E2, 47A7.

[60] Ib. 30C5-8.

[61] Ib. 30D1-31A1, cf. 39E3-4.

[62] Plato, *Meno* 81C9-D4.

[63] For *psyche* in the vegetable world, see *Timaeus* 77A3-B6.

[64] Plato, *Sophist* 240A7-B9.

[65] Ib. 240B9: ἔστι γε μὴν πως.

[66] Ib. 240C1-2: κινδυνεύει τοιαύτην τινὰ πεπλέχθαι συμπλοκὴν τὸ μὴ ὂν τῷ ὄντι.

[67] Ib. 254D4-255E7, esp. 255E3-4. Isolated hints of these Forms appear already in *Parmenides* 143B1-8 and 146D5.

idea behind this is actually quite simple. Being enables us to know the true existence of a given entity, Sameness gives each its identity, and Difference delineates its essential characteristics from those of all other Forms. Thus all three Forms are needed to make anything knowable and identifiable as true, and since true copies, too, are different from their originals, these Forms help us distinguish not only one Form from another, but also to see what is true and what is not true in the visible copy.

With this in mind, we now return to the account of the soul in the *Timaeus*. Since the soul mediates between the indivisible Being of the Forms and the divisible Being that comes into existence in the bodily copies of Forms, the Demiurge fashioned it by first creating from the Being, Sameness, and Difference of the Forms and from the being, sameness, and difference that appears in bodies intermediate kinds of being, sameness, and difference, which he then welded into one entity, the soul.[68] This serves to explain, for example, not only the sameness and differences which soul displays in the motions and orbits of the planets, but also our ability to know them; it also accounts for our ability to differentiate true affirmative from true negative statements and both from false statements.[69]

How does Plato explain the generation of the perceptible things in our world? Since changeless Being cannot be turned into Becoming without undergoing change, Plato interposes between them a kind of transformer, which, as he puts it, has "the power and nature to be the Receptacle of all generation, its nurse, as it were." [70] The Receptacle is itself the passive "matrix for all things,"[71] a recipient which is itself not subject to change. It is the place where generation takes place: "the copies of everlasting entities," that is, copies of Forms,[72] enter it and from them it produces the visible objects of our world, as a mother produces a child from the seed supplied by the father without changing her own identity. And as in the case of a child, the nature of the visible objects consists of the copies of the Forms as combined in the Receptacle,[73] less knowable than the Forms but somehow knowable

---

[68] Plato, *Timaeus* 35A1-B3.

[69] Ib. 37A2-C5.

[70] Ib. 49A4-6.

[71] Ib. 50C2-5.

[72] Loc. cit.

[73] Ib. 50D2-4, E2.

through sense perception and opinion, because copies of ever-lasting entities went into their making.[74]

A comment on these "copies of Forms" which enter the Recep-tacle will help us understand what will later be said in the *Laws* about νόμος and φύσις. They are first and foremost the four ele-ments—earth, fire, air, and water—which had been described as products of divine craftsmanship in the *Sophist*[75] and which the fifth-century natural philosophers had treated as the constituent parts of φύσις and as the causes of all things. For Plato, however, these elements are not knowable, because they constantly change into one another through condensation and rarefaction: condensed water becomes earth, rarefied water becomes air; condensed fire becomes air, condensed air water, which, when condensed, turns into earth again.[76] What enters the Receptacle are, therefore, not irreducible and changeless elements, but only elemental qualities which can be apprehended by true opinion. The elements themselves have true Being only as changeless Forms, "unsleeping and truly existing in nature,"[77] which only the mind can perceive.[78]

With this we can turn to our second question: what is the nature of man and how does it fit into this grand canvas? The immortal part of the human soul which contains mind was fash-ioned by the Demiurge from the less pure leftovers of the world soul, and it is thus inferior, yet akin to the divine.[79] The creation of the human body to house the mortal part of the soul, the seat of irrational desires and appetites, was left by the Demiurge to the conventional gods whom he had created.[80] They lodged the im-mortal mind in the head and spread the mortal soul through the rest of the body, so as to enable each part of the body to fulfil its natural function. Man has thus a dual nature, each in constant conflict with the other, and its weakness is due to the fact that the appetites which have their seat in the body strive for dominance with the appetite for intelligence (φρόνησις) which is located in our divine part, the mind.[81] If we permit our bodily desires to take over,

---

[74] Ib. 52A4-7.
[75] Plato, *Sophist* 266B2-4.
[76] Plato, *Timaeus* 49A6-C7.
[77] Ib. 52B7.
[78] Ib. 51B6-E6.
[79] Ib. 41D4-E1.
[80] Ib. 39E3-40A7, 41B7-C6, 69A6-D6.
[81] Ib. 88A7-B5.

they will implant ignorance in the soul,[82] and mind will be prevented from pursuing those true causes which belong to "the intelligent nature" to which it is akin.[83]

This account of human nature, capable of reaching out through mind to what is everlasting and divine, but at the same time threatened and enfeebled by strong bodily desires, was intended as a preface to a new treatment of human society. So much is suggested by the dramatic setting of the *Timaeus*. It purports to begin where a discussion of institutions, similar to those of the state of the Guardians in the *Republic* had left off the day before,[84] and its account of the nature of the universe, of the world, and of man was to serve as some kind of model to be used by the philosopher of the *Republic* in creating the "state founded in accordance with nature." For, we are told, Critias will follow Timaeus, "taking over from him mankind begotten by his account and from Socrates that portion of it which has received an outstanding education." He will demonstrate that Athens was actually governed on true scientific principles nine thousand years before Solon, when the excellence of her government enabled her to defeat the people of Atlantis; but soon thereafter she was destroyed by earthquakes and floods.[85] The reason why this promised account is given neither in the fragmentary dialogue *Critias* nor in any other later dialogue can be inferred from the *Statesman*, which re-opens the question of the possibility of scientific government among men from a new and somewhat different angle than we find in the *Republic* and with a greater awareness of the weakness of human nature.

The objects of moral knowledge which figured so prominently in the *Republic* play a very secondary role in the *Statesman*. Its main concern is to define the skill (τέχνη) which a statesman or king— the terms are used interchangeably throughout the dialogue— needs for ruling. The first attempt defines this τέχνη as being of the same order as that of the herdsman.[86] But this definition is shown to be wanting through the telling of a myth, according to which, in the distant age of Kronos, the universe was divinely guided, and each province on earth was ruled by a god in the

---

[82] Ib. 86B1-C3.
[83] Ib. 46D5-E1.
[84] Ib. 17A2-C1.
[85] Ib. 27A7-B6.
[86] Plato, *Politicus* 258B3-267C3.

same way in which human shepherds now rule over animals and provide their every need. This age came to an end with earthquakes and destruction of life, when the divine helmsman let go the rudder of the universe and the gods foresook their several provinces on earth. Thus we are now living in an age in which we have to make shift for ourselves, until the god takes pity and resumes control over mankind.[87] In short, the analogy of statesman with herdsman applies to the age of Kronos, but not to our age in which the statesman is like and not naturally superior to his flock.[88] If we bear in mind that Critias, too, wanted to relegate the philosophic rule of the *Republic*, in which the high human potential attributed to human nature by Timaeus is realised, to a distant past, subsequently obliterated by earthquakes and floods, we may well regard the *Statesman* as modifying Plato's faith in the possibility of establishing the absolutely best state here on earth: the actualities of the human situation demand a new and different approach.[89]

The new approach does not, however, lead Plato to the abandonment of his belief in true knowable principles on which scientific government is based. But these principles are referred to only in general terms as ὅροι, "standards," [90] "the truest standard of the right administration of the state," [91] and "the real and original truth itself which is not a copy," [92] and always in contexts in which the knowledge with which the expert statesman governs is favorably compared with the government of states not ruled on scientific principles. In short, concern with objects of knowledge gives way to a stress on the managerial rather than the intellectual qualities of statesmanship. Significantly, an analogy with the weaver is substituted for the rejected analogy with the herdsman. As the weaver's skill depends for its exercise on subsidiary crafts, such as carding, spinning, making of warp and woof, yet is superior to them in that it coordinates them and produces the cloth, so the statesman depends on producers of raw materials and tools and on the services of laborers, merchants, shipowners, and so forth,

---

[87] Ib. 268D5-274E1.
[88] Ib. 274E10-275C5.
[89] Cf. R. Maurer, *Platons "Staat" und die Demokratie* (Berlin, 1970) 167-71.
[90] Plato, *Politicus* 293E1.
[91] Ib. 296E2-3.
[92] Ib. 300E1-2: τοῦτο οὐκ ἔστιν ἔτι μίμημα ἀλλ' αὐτὸ τὸ ἀληθέστατον ἐκεῖνο.

yet his alone is the expert skill of managing the life of the state.[93]
He will be assisted by the orator, the general, and the judge, but
they merely publicise and enforce rules laid down by the statesman;
they do not formulate them.[94] We learn no more than that about
the substantive aspects of the statesman's skill, except that he will
enforce strict marriage laws by weaving the aggressive and courageous warp of society to the quiet and self-controlled weft; like
temperaments will not be permitted to marry one another in order
not to breed an excess, which would destroy the fabric of the
state.[95]

Yet the knowledge and skill of statesmanship are treated as the
only criterion for a right constitution.[96] "It makes no difference
whether their subjects be willing or unwilling; they may rule with
or without a written code of laws, they may be poor or wealthy."[97]
Again we get an analogy with the doctor: just as his science does
not depend on the patient's willingness or unwillingness to accept
painful or unpleasant treatment, as long as the treatment is for
the good of the body, so the expert statesman may banish his
subjects or put them to death, so long as he applies "knowledge and
a standard of justice to preserve and improve the citizenry to the
best of his ability."[98] This, according to Plato, is the only right
constitution; all others are more or less authentic to the degree to
which they imitate the rule of the expert statesman.[99]

Our sensibilities recoil at such authoritarianism. But we must
not forget that it is informed not by arbitrary whims but by an
objective standard of what is true and right.[100] Further, it is
comforting to see our shock echoed in the dialogue in the objection
that a rule without laws is a hard thing to swallow,[101] an objection
which leads straight into a discussion of the nature of law. Although
lawmaking is conceded a place in the royal science of statesmanship,
laws are necessarily inferior to the knowledge which an expert can
flexibly apply to changing situations.[102] Law is too rigid and

---

[93] Ib. 279A7-290E9.
[94] Ib. 303D4-305E7.
[95] Ib. 305E8-311C8.
[96] Ib. 292C8-293A1.
[97] Ib. 293A6-9.
[98] Ib. 293A9-D9.
[99] Ib. 293E1-5.
[100] Ib. 293E1.
[101] Ib. 293E6-7.
[102] Ib. 294A6-8.

inflexible: neither can it foresee and provide for every eventuality that may arise [103] nor does it permit challenges and questions concerning a rule it has once laid down, even if the situation for which it was originally enacted has changed for the better.[104]

Still, the human situation makes it impossible to get along without laws. We cannot count on an expert statesman, a rare phenomenon at any time, to be available at every moment. Plato illustrates this point by the analogy of a doctor who unexpectedly has to go abroad and can no longer attend to his patient in person. He will leave behind written instructions, which will be absolutely binding on the patient, even though they cannot possibly provide for every turn which the patient's condition may undergo. The doctor himself is not bound by his instructions. His expertise entitles him to change the treatment in any way and at any time as he sees fit. Similarly, the expert statesman cannot be bound by the laws he has enacted, if the good of the body politic demands a treatment different from what they enjoin; [105] as a doctor may coerce his patient to submit to his treatment, so a true statesman has the right to use violence, if necessary, to enforce what he knows to be "the truest standard of correct administration of the state." [106] In the absence of a scientific ruler, men will gather together to work out written codes, chasing, as Plato puts it, "to catch the tracks of the truest constitution," [107] even though such laws can at best only imitate "the real and original truth itself," [108] which consists in the knowledge of the expert statesman. Complete loyalty to such laws is the second-best method, the last recourse, and the only hope for good government in the absence of the true statesman. The *Laws*, Plato's last work, takes off from this point: doubting the possibility that human weakness will ever produce an expert statesman, he looks now to a code of laws to embody scientific principles of government.

The superiority of government by the living knowledge of an expert over government by written laws is reaffirmed in the *Laws*.[109] But now even this possibility is relegated to the age of

---

[103] Ib. 294A10-B6.
[104] Ib. 294C1-4.
[105] Ib. 295B10-296A1.
[106] Ib. 296E2-3.
[107] Ib. 301D8-E4.
[108] Ib. 300E1-2.
[109] Plato, *Laws* 9.875C3-D2.

Kronos in a lost past.[110] "Regulation and law" must, as in the *Statesman*, serve as a second best in full awareness that general rules are the best that can be expected from laws.[111] But there is a difference: the *Statesman* made lawgiving subservient to the royal science,[112] but in the *Laws* Plato credits the lawgiver with a τέχνη of his own which provides him with "a truth he can hold on to." [113] That this truth involves the Forms of the moral virtues is not explicitly stated, but it is strongly suggested by other statements made on the activity of the lawgiver: he will be guided by a vision of virtue as a whole; [114] he will look at the standard of justice and injustice in framing laws for the benefit of the community; [115] and it is finally expressed in the assumption, at the end of the *Laws*, that the members of the Nocturnal Council, to whom the general supervision of the state and further legislation is to be entrusted, will themselves have undergone the kind of education which had been prescribed for the philosopher in the *Republic*.[116] In other words, Plato now recognises that neither a philosopher nor an expert statesman is indispensable for government based on true knowledge of absolute moral principles; laws, too, if properly framed, can bring science to bear on the government of men.

What goes into the proper framing of a law? Good legislation cannot be as harsh as the expert statesman was permitted to be. It must not simply coerce the citizens to do certain things and refrain from doing others, but it must first explain to them the need for a given law and persuade them to accept it.[117] Accordingly, each major law is to be preceded by a preamble which will educate the citizens by persuasion.[118]

The discussion which serves as a preamble to the laws against impiety in the tenth book is often regarded—and rightly so—as the metaphysical preamble to the *Laws* as a whole. Its additional importance for us is that it contains Plato's definitive and most profound statement on the relation of law and nature. In form it is a

---

110 Ib. 4.713A6-E3, 9.853C3-6.
111 Ib. 9.875D2-5.
112 Plato, *Politicus* 294A6-8.
113 Plato, *Laws* 4.709C8: ἀληθείας ἐχόμενον.
114 Ib. 3.688B1, 4.714B8-C1: πρὸς πᾶσαν ‹ἀρετὴν› βλέπειν.
115 Ib. 4.714B6-7, 715B4.
116 Ib. 12.968C3-969D3 with H. Cherniss in *Gnomon* 25 (1953) 373-4, 377-9.
117 Ib. 4.720A2-E6.
118 Ib. 4.722C6-723B8, 9.858B6-859B5.

refutation of views on φύσις proposed by the natural philosophers of
the fifth century, which, Plato believes, lie at the root of much of
the godlessness and immorality to which especially young people
are prone, when they have first been exposed to what seem to them
new and revolutionary ideas. It will be recalled that Plato had attacked the natural philosophers before in his account of the generation
of the perceptible world in the *Timaeus*, where he had challenged
their view that the four elements and their qualities of hot and
cold, solid and liquid, hard and soft, are the irreducible constituent
parts of nature and the cause of all generation. The same attack is
renewed in the *Laws* with a different and sharper thrust. In regarding the elements and their random motions and combinations
as the primary cause of all generation, the natural philosophers
attribute the existence of all things to nature and chance. Expert
skill (τέχνη) is for them something practised by mere men; its
products are derivative and secondary in that they depend on the
bodies produced by primary generation to supply the raw materials
for skill. Legislation is, on this view, entirely the product of human
skill and, since it is as derivative as any other skill, it is based not
on nature but on unverifiable assumptions.[119] Moreover, the fact
that different beliefs about the gods are held in different places
and that laws differ from place to place is taken as evidence that
the gods as well as the laws are products of human skill and have
no existence in nature. Further, moral values cannot be derived
from nature: what is honorable by nature is not honorable by
law; what is just would not be open to constant disputes if it were
sanctioned by nature. The moral consequences are that whatever
violent action one can get away with is regarded as just;[120] the
right kind of life is to follow nature, "to live as master over others
and not, as the law bids, as a slave to others." [121] The echoes of
Callicles are unmistakable in this account of the teaching of the
natural philosophers and the attitudes to which they lead.

The requirements for a satisfactory refutation are outlined by
Cleinias: the lawgiver must, through persuasion, "come to the aid
of ancient law by arguing that the gods and (all that is honorable,
just, and great) do exist; he must rise to the defense of law itself and
of expert skill as existing by nature or as not inferior to nature,

---

[119] Ib. 10.888E4-889E1.
[120] Cf. also ib. 4.714B6-715A2 with 2.690B8-C3.
[121] Ib. 10.889E3-890A9.

inasmuch as right reason affirms them to be creations of mind." [122]
The challenge is taken up by the proof of a factor which had been
ignored in the materialist accounts of nature: the primacy of
soul over body. If soul, whose most fundamental characteristic
is to move itself and to impart motion to everything else,[123] is
prior to body, it—and not chance—will be the determinant cause
of all changes and transformations of bodies; and further, whatever
belongs to soul will be prior to all material things.[124] This means
that expert skill, law, and mind, which belong to soul, will be prior
to such material qualities as hardness, softness, heaviness, and
lightness. Again, if the name φύσις properly belongs to whatever is
primary, it belongs to soul and not, as the natural philosophers
want, to the elements and their qualities. For since the elements
depend for their motions on soul, they are secondary, and the
bodies they create depend not on chance combinations but on the
expert skill and mind that are inherent in soul.[125] What is first
stated as a hypothesis is soon substantiated by the proof that
"soul is identical with the primary generation of what is, was, and
will be," since it is "the cause of all change and motion in all
things;" [126] "it came to be before the body, and the body is secondary and later, by nature subject to the rule of soul." [127]

I hope my brief summary has not made Plato's argument un-
intelligible. What that argument has achieved, apart from establishing the priority of soul as the source of all motion over matter
or body, is (1) to reject the view of φύσις held by the natural philosophers in favor of a φύσις dominated by soul, and (2) to make τέχνη,
law, and mind as properties of soul share in its priority over matter.

It remains to explore the consequences of this for the relation
of νόμος and φύσις to one another. Plato gives no explicit account of
what he means by "nature" in the Laws. But there is at least one
passage which suggests that he means by it what the Timaeus
had described as "the nature of the universe," [128] which is eternal
and includes all Forms,[129] and which had contributed Being and

---

[122] Ib. 10.890D4-7.
[123] Ib. 10.895E10-896B3.
[124] Ib. 10.892A2- B1.
[125] Ib. 10.892B3-C7.
[126] Ib. 10.896A6-B1.
[127] Ib. 10.896C1-3.
[128] Plato, Timaeus 41E2, 47A7.
[129] Ib. 37D3, 38B8, 39E2; 28A6-B1.

the φύσις of Sameness and of Difference to the world soul [130]
through which that mind was implanted in living creatures which
makes the true Being of the Forms accessible to them.[131] In any
event, I can think of no other view of φύσις which would account
for the priority of soul over matter and at the same time of mind
over matter.

I find it somewhat harder to explain how Plato envisaged law
and τέχνη to share in the priority of soul, because his view can
only be inferred from statements scattered throughout the *Laws*.
We have already seen that the lawgiver possesses an expert skill [132]
through which he can imitate the rule of Kronos in which no laws
were needed.[133] We also saw that he "clings to the truth" in
enacting his laws,[134] and that he models them on "virtue as a
whole," [135] on "that which is always beautiful," [136] and on "the
just and the unjust." [137] We are, further, told that he "must not
only be able to look toward the many details, but must strive
toward knowledge of the one central object to organise in its
light all the details he has encompassed in one view." [138] This
kind of language, it seems to me, makes the conclusion inescapable
that the moral Forms, on the knowledge of which the "state
founded in accordance with nature" was based in the *Republic*
and which were part of the nature of the universe in the *Timaeus*,
are now thought of as accessible to the mind of the lawgiver and
as embodied through his expert skill in the laws he will enact.
That this is the right interpretation is confirmed in some measure
by a statement in *Laws* 12: "Of all studies that which is probably
most decisive in making the student a better person is the study
of the laws, provided they are rightly framed; else it would be to
no purpose that law, a divine and admirable institution for us
bears a name proper to mind." [139] The law-mind relation is based on
the pun νόμος-νόος, which English cannot recapture. That Plato

---

[130] Ib. 35A1-B3.
[131] Cf. Plato, *Laws* 12.961D7-962B2 for νοῦς in ψυχή seeing the σκοπός of a
τέχνη and providing σωτηρία.
[132] Ib. 9.875A5-6, B2-3.
[133] Ib. 4.709C1-D2; 9.875A5-6.
[134] Ib. 4.709C8.
[135] Ib. 3.688B1, cf. 12.962D1-5.
[136] Ib. 4.706A2.
[137] Ib. 4.714B6-7; cf. 9.875C1.
[138] Ib. 12.965B7-10.
[139] Ib. 12.957C4-7.

was not merely playful in coining it but believed the similarity of words to reflect a true relationship between law and mind is suggested by its recurrence in three other passages in the *Laws*, in one of which it is extended to define νόμος as the διανομή (dispensation) of νοῦς.[140] Law, accessible to mind and actualised through the expert skill of the lawgiver, thus belongs to that soul which has been fashioned from the eternal and transcendent nature of the universe. Through soul, law is a part of that nature, dispensed by the mind which works in it and apprehended through the kinship of all nature by our mind, which is the immortal part of what we have of soul. Despite the concessions he had to make to human weakness, and despite his increasing doubts, first that a philosopher, and second that an expert statesman would ever emerge to establish a society based on true and knowable moral principles, Plato never abandoned his conviction in the existence of such a science; he merely realised that its application is more safely left to laws rooted in a transcendental knowable nature than to frail human beings.

---

[140] Ib. 4.714A1-2, cf. 2.674B7 and 8.836E4.

# DIALECTIC, MYTH AND HISTORY IN THE PHILOSOPHY OF PLATO

## JOHN F. CALLAHAN

In a symposium celebrating the twenty-fourth centenary of Plato's birth I have thought it might be appropriate to discuss some features of his philosophy that seem to me of central importance to his philosophical method, and likewise to attempt, with regard to these same features, to relate him, perforce sketchily, both to the earlier tradition and to those of his successors on whom his influence has been most striking.[1]

The impact made in the last hundred years by the ever-increasing interest in myth on the study of philosophy is in itself a topic that would require detailed examination. It touches of course upon the problem of the origins and early development of philosophy as we know it in the Western world. But, transcending the purely historical question of the way in which this philosophy came to be, it provides us with illumination on the nature of philosophy itself, compelling us to examine what we really mean by philosophy and how we conceive it to be related to those other fields, such as natural science and theology, in which the human mind poses its most searching questions.

Because the evidence for the origins of philosophy is so limited—though any number of elaborate constructions have been based on it—the historian of early Greek philosophy may be cautious today in his employment of myth to explain the beginnings of philosophy, but he is not likely to reject a causal role for myth with the same confidence as did John Burnet at the turn of the century.[2] On the other hand, even the one who sees a close relationship between early philosophy and its mythical predecessors will usually hesitate to work out the details of his view with the enthusiasm of F. M. Cornford.[3] But even if one looks at the more

---

[1] I wish to acknowledge gratefully the cooperation of the National Endowment for the Humanities in providing time for a research project of which the present essay is a part.

[2] *Early Greek Philosophy* [4] (London, 1930), pp. 13-18.

[3] Note especially the Preface of *From Religion to Philosophy* (New York, 1957), pp. v-x.

recent and more sober appraisal of Werner Jaeger that "it is not easy to say how the Homeric idea that Ocean is the origin of everything differs from the doctrine of Thales that water is the basic principle of the universe: for Thales' theory was certainly inspired by the tangible reality of the inexhaustible sea," [4] we may still ask whether Thales' view was inspired only by looking at the vast expanse of the sea from the shore of Miletus with or without a possible influence exerted on him by the ancient reverence paid to water in the guise of Ocean. If the older mythical view and the newer one of Thales were both inspired by the readily observed power of the element water, as seems very plausible, does it follow that we would look in vain for something different in the doctrine of Thales? Aristotle, after all, calls him the first of the philosophers with explicit reference to his choice of water as the source of all things.[5] This point is indeed crucial, since presumably a philosopher may make statements that could also be made by someone else, a theologian or a scientist or even the man in the street, but nevertheless preserve his distinctiveness because of the special motivation and method he employs. Without determining here precisely what a philosophical method is, aside from the requirement that it be somehow rational—with or without non-rational elements involved—we must admit that such a method came into existence in the Greek world, and there is no good reason to deny that it could have existed as early as Thales.

The problem of determining how distinctively philosophical Thales and his immediate successors may have been, as opposed to their more myth-loving predecessors and contemporaries, really arises from a lack of evidence regarding the kind of tradition to which they belong and the precise position they occupy within that tradition. It is tempting to look upon Hesiod, with his curious mixture of the mythical and the rational, as a transitional figure between the older mythical approach to an explanation of reality and the newer scientific and philosophical one. A transitional figure he doubtless is, but his uniqueness in this respect may be due in large measure to the absence of literary evidence to the contrary, that is, to an accident of transmission.

Similarly with Thales, whom Aristotle and we accept as the first philosopher, we may wonder whether his philosophical approach,

---

4 *Paideia: the Ideals of Greek Culture*, I (Oxford, 1939), 149.
5 *Metaph.* A.3.983B20-21.

whatever it may consist in, could not have been anticipated by some philosophical predecessors, undocumented even in the ancient world, who offered their speculations in a tradition running parallel to the more mythical one. We have no really appropriate analogies from elsewhere to help us here, and the constructions made by various scholars of the manner in which the scientific tradition came to succeed or to be separated from the mythical one depend too often on a particular view of what the relation in general between philosophy and myth or religion is or should be, with an almost irresistible temptation to project such a view into the long-distant past.

Throughout the early period of philosophy our attention is being constantly directed by the philosophers themselves to the possible role that myth may play in their thinking, but almost always in a very ambiguous way. When Heraclitus, for example, says that the wise is unwilling and willing to be called by the name of Zeus,[6] we may interpret this as meaning that Heraclitus' first principle, arrived at by a new scientific method, is not the anthropomorphic deity espoused by the older religion but nevertheless holds in this reformed hierarchy a comparable position of primacy. That is to say, Heraclitus may simply be offering a manifesto of philosophy's independence from a religious way of thinking. But who can tell how far his willingness to accept the name of Zeus may carry along with it a mythical content at least by way of connotation?

When we arrive at Empedocles we may consider ourselves to be in a position to balance the mythical and rational motivations of an early Greek philosopher, even though our information falls short of what we might reasonably require. If we look at the two poems that have come down to us, though in a very fragmentary condition, *On nature* and *Purifications*, we see what may be a fairly clear division between the scientific approach to the problem of nature and the largely mythical treatment of the life of man. There can be no real doubt about the scientific legitimacy of the four elements employed by Empedocles in the poem *On nature*, if only because—in the transformation brought about by Aristotle— they long withstood the pragmatic test of time in the field of natural philosophy down to the period of modern philosophy and

---

[6] Frag. 32 (Diels-Kranz [6], from which all citations of the Pre-Socratics are taken).

science. On the other hand, the view of man, not as a soul but a *daimon* whose existence transcends the short-lived union with the body, is clearly in the mythical tradition that we have come to associate with the mystery-religions.[7]

Yet the separation of the two realms is by no means complete in Empedocles. The four elements in the poem *On nature* are given mythological names,[8] though there may be a strongly conventional reason for this, and the motive power of Love[9] is certainly reminiscent of the Eros of Hesiod. More important are the indications in the *Purifications* that the vicissitudes suffered by the *daimon* are in some way coordinated with the cycle of mixture and separation of the elements in nature. Strife brings about the fall of the *daimon* from its original abode and also acts in nature to separate the elements from one another; the fallen *daimon* is buffeted by each of the four elements in turn, being passed on forcibly from one to another as a stage in the expiation of its primeval crime.[10] In Empedocles we meet a philosopher whose explicit use of materials taken from a mythical source can be related to a purpose that may be called philosophical. We can indeed say that the union—however imperfect in itself and enigmatic for us it may be—of the philosophical and the mythical in Empedocles has set a precedent the importance of which in the subsequent history of thought would be hard to calculate.

But how are we to look at Empedocles? Is he a shaman who turns up rather improbably on the southern coast of Sicily, detaching himself from his mythological lore to the extent of elaborating a scientific doctrine that has met widespread acceptance? Or is he rather a scientific thinker who at some point rebels against subjecting man to the ironbound rigors of a system that constantly becomes stronger and more constraining to all human aspirations? Whichever is the case, it is the mythical part of Empedocles' thought that sets man apart from the nature of things as a whole, since the elements that make up his being are shared with everything else in the universe. His life cannot be explained in terms of such universal elements and the moving

---

[7] It is not necessary to discuss here the question about the relative contributions of the mystery-religions and the Pythagoreans to the doctrine of the soul's preexistence and immortality.

[8] Frag. 6.

[9] Frag. 17.

[10] Frag. 115.

powers that are responsible for their mixture and separation. The
life of man as we observe it makes sense only if we look upon it as
a pilgrimage and an expiation. As Empedocles says of himself,
"I too am now one of these, an exile from the gods and a wanderer." [11] Though he clearly belongs to a scientific and philosophical
tradition, he has utilized pre-existing religious and mythical
materials to give human life a significance that transcends the
world around it, however much it may share—at least in its present
condition—the natural causes that operate in that world. It is
this duality of approach—whatever underlying unity there may
be—that makes Empedocles an archetypal figure in the philosophy
of man, though it remains for Plato to carry on his work in such
a way as to give it a permanent influence in the subsequent history
of thought.

It may seem superfluous, or even foolhardy, to take up once
more the mythical element in Plato after so many and such diverse
treatments have been accorded it. But the subject is of such basic
importance both for the interpretation of Plato and for an understanding in general of the relation between philosophy and myth
that an attempt to approach it once again may be forgiven. I
should like to point to three aspects of the mythmaker's art in
Plato, and in particular three ways in which he uses myth in the
service of his dialectic, which is the essence of his philosophizing.

In the first place, there are those myths that do not contain
dialectical elements, at least in an overt way, but offer a mythical
treatment of a subject that has been treated dialectically, giving a
mythical counterpart of the dialectic or even going beyond the
area covered by the dialectic. Toward the beginning of the *Timaeus*
there is a summary of a portion of the argument of the *Republic*,
and we are then told that this kind of argument provides us with a
picture of the ideal state but a picture in which there is no motion.
Just as someone, Socrates says, on seeing beautiful figures, either
created by art or actually living but immobile, desires to see them
engaged in some kind of motion that is suitable to them, so he
would gladly listen to anyone who would take the state he has
described and show how it wages war against other states, ex-
hibiting in its actions qualities that accord with its education and
training.[12] To portray concretely the state outlined in the *Republic*,

---

[11] *Ibid.*
[12] *Tim.* 17C-20C.

with especial attention to its setting itself in motion for the purpose
of waging war, we are then given in the *Timaeus* the myth of
ancient Athens and the fabled city Atlantis,[13] which is set forth
more fully in the *Critias*. Similarly, after the arguments for the
immortality of the soul in the *Phaedo* there is a myth in which the
fate of the soul in the life to come is described and the different
destinies of the good and the bad soul are set apart. Socrates
expresses diffidence in his ability to prove that his account of the
wonderful regions of the earth is true, and at the end he asserts
that a sensible man would not maintain that everything is just as
he has recounted it. Nevertheless, he adds, it would be a worthy
venture to believe this account or something like it, since the
soul does appear to be immortal; for the venture is a good one.[14]
Myths like these are easily recognizable and have long since been
classified by such terms as eschatological or aetiological. Even
though there has been general acknowledgment that such myths
are not merely ornamental but are an integral part of Plato's
philosophizing, there has been a tendency to follow the distinction
made long ago by J. A. Stewart, who speaks of "the characteristics
and influence of Plato the Mythologist, or Prophet, as distinguished
from Plato the Dialectician, or Reasoner." [15] But, for reasons I
hope to make clear a little later, I think that this distinction,
harmless as it may seem, is likely to be a superficial, if not an
actually misleading, view of these, the most easily recognizable
of the Platonic myths.

There is a second kind of myth, one in which it would be very
difficult to distinguish the mythical components from the dialectic
itself, one example of which is the cosmogonical myth that occupies
most of the *Timaeus*. In the course of this myth we come across
many of the elements of dialectic found throughout the dialogues,
such as the contrast of being and becoming and of knowledge and
opinion, the use of intelligible models, and different kinds of
imitation. Most striking perhaps is the recurrence of a favorite
Platonic device, that is, changing the number of terms employed in
the course of a dialectical discussion. In the *Timaeus* the most
important transition is signaled by a shift from a two-term to a
three-term dialectic, and we are told explicitly—which does not

---

[13] *Tim.* 20E-26E.
[14] *Phaedo* 107B-115A.
[15] *The Myths of Plato* (London, 1905), p. v.

always happen when Plato makes such a shift—that we have exhausted the possibilities of the two terms that have hitherto been used and in order to go farther we must introduce a third. At the beginning of Timaeus' discourse we are offered the two terms that we are told are required, being and becoming, and these are employed to set forth the works of Reason in the production of the universe. Later we find that in taking up the works of Necessity these two are no longer sufficient. In addition to being and becoming, which may now be called the model and the copy, we need a third term, which turns out to be the receptacle in which becoming takes place.[16] Through the use of this third term we are able to penetrate farther into the world of appearances and to separate the role of space, which is identified with the receptacle in the realm of Necessity, from that of time, which we have learned earlier is an instrument of Reason in the process of ordering the universe.[17] The fresh start that Timaeus makes by adding a third term as he turns from Reason to Necessity is a dialectical device that may be paralleled elsewhere, as —to take only one example—in the sequence of speeches in the *Symposium*. (It is surely not a mere historical reaction on the part of Plato, as Wilamowitz once suggested,[18] to the sudden perusal of Democritus' works containing a theory of nature that Plato felt obliged to confront with one of his own.) If we may indeed distinguish the dialectical and the mythical in such a treatment as that of the *Timaeus*, we see that each in turn propels the other, and the two elements complement each other so aptly and are so thoroughly intertwined that the result is a perfect fusion of the two.

Although lip service is almost universally paid to the mythical character of Timaeus' discourse, the dialogue has, for all practical purposes, served as a mine to be exploited by anyone who wishes to build up a Platonic system of literal doctrine and find substantiation for his particular system in this dialogue. Yet this can be done only by violating some of the most obvious rules of consistency. One example will suffice. At the beginning of his description of the soul of the universe Timaeus tells us that this soul was

---

[16] *Tim.* 48E-49A.

[17] *Tim.* 37C-39E.

[18] *Platon* (Berlin, 1919), II, 258-265, where his point of departure is a proposal of Ingeborg Hammer-Jensen. A. E. Taylor disagrees with this for his own special reasons, *A Commentary on Plato's Timaeus* (Oxford, 1928), pp. 3, 298.

spread evenly throughout the body of the spherical universe and even overlapped it a little on the outside. We are then presented with a picture of the soul's substance as being shaped into two long strips which are formed into circles so that they touch each other at two points, one of these circles representing the stable course of the heaven of fixed stars, the other, divided into seven smaller circles, providing the orbits of the sun, the moon and the five known planets. After concluding this section with a description of the varying motions of the seven smaller circles, Timaeus in the very next sentences returns to the picture of the soul as being woven throughout the universe from center to circumference and enveloping it from without.[19] It is clear that he has two pictures of the soul firmly in view, and we cannot claim that when he offers us one of them the other has slipped his mind. The two different descriptions cannot both be meant literally, of course. At least one of them must be figurative, but which? There is no indication in the text by which one rather than the other can be accepted as a literal statement, so that both must be understood in a figurative sense. But if the shape or shapes of the soul are figurative, not literal, what of the components that are said to enter into the constitution of the soul and the process by which it is made by the divine craftsman? What then of the very existence of the soul of the universe and of the craftsman himself, of whom we have earlier been told that to discover him would indeed be a task, and, if we should discover him, to tell all men about him would be impossible? [20] The text of the *Timaeus* offers us no pretext for drawing a line between the figurative and the literal, that is, for lifting elements out of the myth to be accepted as literal doctrine. It is a seamless fabric, and we make such distinctions in it only at the risk of being capricious, of utterly neglecting the way in which dialectic and myth are so completely fused in the dialogue.[21]

Even in a dialogue like the *Phaedo*, in which a myth of some length is set apart from the dialectical argumentation, mythical elements are mixed with the dialectic and, in effect, form a not unimportant part of it. The most striking of these is perhaps the employment—one of the many in Plato—of the myth of the soul's

---

[19] *Tim.* 34B-36E.

[20] *Tim.* 28C.

[21] A typical attempt to separate a literal doctrine from the myth of the *Timaeus* is that of R. Hackforth, "Plato's Cosmogony (*Timaeus* 27D ff.)," *Classical Quarterly*, IX (1959), 17-22.

preexistence,[22] which he takes over from predecessors such as Empedocles. If it is a traditional myth of the soul's preexistence that our dialectic examines in order to make an inference about its post-existence or immortality, we should consider whether the immortality to which we have argued is not still in the realm of the mythical and cannot be meant literally, and whether, once again, as in the *Timaeus*, the dialectical and the mythical are not two sides of the same coin. As long as I have raised here a point that may even at this date be controversial, I may as easily add another, namely, the use of the theory of ideas in the *Phaedo*, our knowledge of which indicates to us that the soul must be like them and therefore immortal.[23] The *Phaedrus* shows us how the theory of ideas may be joined with that of the soul's preexistence in a fully-developed myth, and the arguments of the *Parmenides* point to the absurdities into which one falls by taking the theory of ideas literally,[24] arguments in which Plato himself anticipates future critics of the ideas. It seems to me very difficult to justify any kind of literal acceptance of the ideas in the *Phaedo*—or elsewhere, and the argument for immortality based on the ideas should be reckoned as another instance of the close union of myth, or at least of a mythical element, and dialectic to form a whole in which a distinction cannot easily be made.

A third purpose of Plato's mythmaking is to provide a setting for the dialectic, and here I refer to the construction of the dialogue itself. If we recognize Plato's ability to produce myths that help to extend the boundaries of his dialectic and myths that even merge into the dialectic itself, should we stop short of granting him the skill to produce a mythical framework that is congenial to the free operation of this method in a great variety of applications? I suggest that each dialogue of Plato is a myth and as such no less important for an understanding of his philosophy and the role of myth in it than the types of myth already mentioned. There might seem to be a difficulty in that the characters who participate in the dialogues are as a whole historical figures, whose existence and many of whose activities can be corroborated from other sources. This is especially true of Socrates, the chief character in the dialogues, the picture of whom presented therein as the philosopher

---

[22] *Phaedo* 72E-73A.
[23] *Phaedo* 78C-79E.
[24] *Parm.* 130A-135C.

who lives and dies in accordance with his philosophical principles has been an inspiration to countless numbers of men from the time of Plato to our own. Very few scholars have gone as far as John Burnet and A. E. Taylor in looking at the dialogues as documents that are basically historical, and in ascribing to Socrates a good deal of the philosophical doctrine usually reserved to Plato. But almost all tend to make concessions, however surreptitiously this is done, to some kind of historical standard to which even Plato must presumably conform. This can take a number of forms, one of which is finding a development from the so-called earlier dialogues to the later ones according to which there is a change from the more Socratic to the more Platonic, though it is difficult to define what these terms mean in such a context without arguing in a circle. Another is to say that certain doctrines and certain events could not have been represented by Plato as different from what was historically true, since friends of Socrates would still have been alive to protest any discrepancy, especially if it concerned such a sensitive subject as the trial, imprisonment and death of their martyred friend.

Such difficulties, however, arise from a misunderstanding of the way in which Plato looks at myth and history. In analyzing the phenomena that take place in a changing universe Plato makes a distinction between Reason and Necessity, which is similar to that between being and becoming or intelligible and sensible, but is more directly related to the causal operations we observe. In the economy of the universe Reason acts according to a pattern and for a good purpose, whereas Necessity, the "wandering cause," comprises all the subsidiary causes that must be "persuaded" by Reason to act for a purpose since they are in themselves indifferent. Myth and history are both in the realm of Necessity because they recount events in which various subsidiary causes are operating, causes that may have been, but just as well may not have been, "persuaded" by Reason.[25] History is of value insofar as it may offer itself as a myth, like any other myth, to the uses of dialectic. A given event in history, even if we can be sure of it, has taken place only once; but that same event, looked on as myth, has taken place many times, and the truth it communicates to us

---

[25] Some illuminating remarks on this subject may be found in Richard McKeon, *Thought, Action and Passion* (Chicago and London, 1954), pp. 75-78.

does not require historical proof and is not limited to a single occurrence. There is an interesting exchange between Socrates and Critias in the *Timaeus*. Critias says that the city which Socrates had previously described as it were in a myth, referring to the *Republic*, will be transported into historical fact, that is, the story of Atlantis. Socrates replies that it is of great importance that Critias is offering, not a myth he has invented, but authentic history.[26] We may wonder, of course, how far the details of the story of Atlantis are historical or are considered so by Critias and his listeners, or, what is more to the point, by Plato and his contemporaries. There is no way in which we can know this on the basis of internal evidence (unless we maintain strongly the historical verisimilitude of the dialogues). New evidence from an external source, however, is always possible, as from the archaeological researches that are being conducted on the Aegean island of Thera and in the Cretan city of Zakros.[27] But even if the most optimistic hopes of scholars are fully realized, and an Aegean locale is generally accepted as the fabled Atlantis, with the details of Critias' story largely substantiated, the question is still before us how far the story serves the philosophical purpose of Plato. We shall find, I think, that regardless of the information we are supplied about the lost Atlantis by the archaeological journals the story still functions as a myth, and as such it supplements and confirms the dialectical construction of the ideal state in the *Republic* (a construction, we should observe, that is referred to, in the *Timaeus*, not as dialectic, but as itself a kind of myth).

The many events that made up the life of the historical Socrates were for Plato, like all history and all myth, in the realm of Necessity, just as much as if he had been a figure out of Greek mythology. For the purposes of Plato's philosophy those events had to be transformed into myth and used in conjunction with other myths, such as those of the soul's preexistence and the creation of the universe, to fit his dialectical method. Understandably anxious as we may be to learn more about the historical figure that underlies the most important personage in the dialogues, this anxiety should not lead us to ask questions of Plato that he does not intend to

---

[26] *Tim.* 26C-E.

[27] Interesting accounts of these researches are N. Platon, *Zakros: The Discovery of a Lost Palace of Ancient Crete* (New York, 1971), pp. 303-320, and A. G. Galanopoulos, *The Truth behind the Legend* (Indianapolis, 1969).

answer and in fact cannot answer in the kind of writing he has undertaken. Information about the historical Socrates must come to us from some other source, and we must be sure that this source understands history as we do and is able to answer the questions in the way we propose them. Whatever Plato may have owed to the historical Socrates in method or in doctrine, we can be sure that the dialectical method we discern in the dialogues is Plato's, and it is a method that is intended to communicate to us, as far as we may be affected by it, philosophical knowledge, which belongs to the realm of Reason, not historical or mythical opinion, which is in the sphere where Necessity holds sway. The dialogue is myth rather than history, but it is also dialectic utilizing myth in the pursuit of truth. The dialectical construction of the ideal state in the *Republic*, like many elements of the dialogues, has been interpreted historically. But, whatever historical background may have existed, such a passage is dialectical, and even mythical—if we accept the description given in the *Timaeus*—and historical events may be retrieved from it—as from any Platonic dialogue—only doubtfully and at the cost of distorting the purpose and method of the philosopher. Similarly, as it seems to me, the setting provided for his dialectic by Plato, that is, the dialogue itself, may well contain historical elements but it is really a form of myth devised by Plato for a particular kind of philosophizing.

The employment of myth in Plato is not only adapted to the purposes of his dialectical method, however, but may even be considered an extension of it. His elaboration of a non-literal use of language, of a logic in which the copula has the meaning "is like" or "is as it were," of a system of analogizing that finds significant likenesses everywhere—all this leads naturally to the widespread use of myths or "likely stories." When he fashioned the dialogue, inspired perhaps by the mimes of the Sicilians Sophron and Xenarchus,[28] he turned it into a literary form perfectly adapted to the employment of dialectic and myth that he must have chosen at an early age to be his characteristic method. The three uses of myth in relation to dialectic that I have distinguished, namely, summing up or extending a dialectical argument, joining and in a

---

[28] In Aristotle *Poet.* 1447B9-11 the two are mentioned in conjunction with "the Socratic dialogues." Plato's interest in Sophron is frequently alluded to by ancient authors, as Quintilian 1.10.17 and Diogenes Laertius 3.18.

sense becoming part of it, and providing a setting in which it can take place—all these are only facets of a basic view of the nature and efficacy of myth, a view that depended on a lively mythical tradition of which Plato and his readers were a part but also on the peculiar genius with which he reacted to that tradition and shaped it to his own purposes so effectively that he gave a permanent impress to the uses of myth in philosophy.

The philosophical employment of myth and history that is specifically Platonic can be made clearer through a comparison of Plato with some of his successors, especially his pupil Aristotle, in whom the contrasts with the method of Plato are particularly illuminating.

If Plato's choice of non-literal language for philosophical analysis and communication facilitates, one might even say demands, the employment of myth, it is just as true that Aristotle's insistence on the literal use of language has a corollary in the relatively infrequent appearance of myth in his works and a very different attitude towards it when it does occur. For Aristotle myth is an object of dialectical examination, to be sure, but dialectic for him has a different role and a much more limited one than it does for Plato. Aristotle, for example, offers a dialectical evaluation of earlier views as a preliminary to his own proper analysis of a problem, and sometimes a myth tells us what men have thought in the past even on scientific and philosophical questions. Underlying the attention that he gives his predecessors is a view of history according to which the same opinions appear in cycles infinitely often.[29] These opinions may be embodied in myths, as he points out when talking of his theory of the heavenly spheres. In the course of history, during which the arts and sciences have developed and then perished, some opinions are preserved like relics of the ancient treasure.[30] It is interesting to note that Plato says that some myths, like that of Phaethon, preserve traces of real events in human memory,[31] and a writer of popular science has utilized this myth for precisely the same purpose.[32]

The relation of myth to history and to philosophy in Aristotle

---

[29] *Meteor.* 1.3.339B27-30.
[30] *Metaph.* Λ.8.1074A38-B13.
[31] *Tim.* 22C-D.
[32] I. Velikovsky, *Worlds in Collision* (New York, 1950), pp. 143-146, 159-160.

differs from that found in Plato in correspondence with his use of literal rather than non-literal language. History is differentiated from myth in a way that is not possible for Plato because history is a literal account of events that have actually occurred at a given time and place, and his acceptance of the efficacy of individual causes in the processes of history leads him on occasion to a kind of writing that we today could term historical. When the *Constitution of Athens* was recovered from the sands of Egypt less than a century ago it was a boon to ancient historians such as no newly-discovered dialogue of Plato could ever be. On the other hand, in its relation to philosophy myth can offer only a resemblance; the lover of myth, we read, is in some sense a lover of wisdom.[33] For the myth, with its employment of non-literal language and its mere adumbration of true philosophical causality, falls far short of the rigorous and systematic exploitation of human wonder that Aristotle expects of philosophy.

In the use that philosophy makes of both history and myth there are differences in Plato and Aristotle that spring from their respective methods of philosophizing but also certain similarities. For Plato history and myth, generally without distinction, may be employed to yield us philosophical truth if we approach them with the correct dialectical method. But for Aristotle history, dealing as it does with individual events, can give us only probability, not the truth that philosophy, with its gaze on the universal, is seeking. Though myth claims a kind of universality not found in history—and Plato acknowledges this claim—it has for Aristotle no sense of the proper philosophical procedure or use of language that alone can lead to the discovery and formulation of truth. History and myth do not enter so directly into the precincts of philosophy as Plato would permit, but they are valuable for Aristotle as an adjunct to philosophy, and this is especially true when we are concerned with the realm of ideas, where Aristotle exhibits his chief interest in these fields. In history and myth he finds evidence, not of the truth of things as such, as Plato does, but only of what men have thought about the truth, and some of their opinions have survived in myth even the destruction of past civilizations. Aristotle conceives his method to be genuinely new in the history of philosophy and the philosophy that results from it has been anticipated only in part and imperfectly in earlier

---

[33] *Metaph.* A.2.982B18-19.

thought. To make the nature of his own philosophy especially
clear Aristotle can schematize the history of previous philosophy
in such a way that Plato occupies a position opposite to that of
"materialists" like Democritus, with Aristotle himself advancing
to a new position, where of course the truth is to be found.[34]
Thus, helpful as history and myth are in the pursuit of scientific
truth, they both—and especially myth—occupy a very subordinate
position in the Aristotelian as compared with the Platonic scheme
of philosophizing.

A special application of the Platonic view of history as opposed
to that of Aristotle may be found in the use Plato makes of the
thought of his predecessors. In evaluating the so-called accuracy
of the two in this respect, scholars commonly express a preference
for Plato, though the reasons are not always to his credit. He is
said, for example, to have caught the spirit of his predecessors'
thought, while Aristotle pays attention only to the letter, and even
then "distorts" their statements to fit the requirements of his own
philosophy. It is not easy to assess the relative merits of Plato and
Aristotle in this area since, for reasons that are mostly accidental,
Plato uses thinkers for whom we have far fewer remains than are
available for those who are reported by Aristotle. But if we were
in a position to check Plato's account against the actual words of
the men he writes about with the same facility that we enjoy
with Aristotle, we would find, I think, that Plato in his own way is
just as likely to be guilty of "distortion" as Aristotle is. Of course,
neither philosopher distorts the views of his predecessors but,
like any creative philosopher discussing another philosopher,
each does this insofar as the other philosopher can contribute
something to the specific way of philosophizing that the reporting
philosopher has elaborated as his own. If we impose our historical
standards on Aristotle and find a discrepancy between the text
of Empedocles or Anaxagoras and what Aristotle says about them,
we should be prepared to find a discrepancy likewise, though of
another kind, between the historical Socrates or Protagoras and
their representations in Plato. But this discrepancy is precisely
the measure of the respective ambitions of Plato and Aristotle,
of Aristotle to find statements that may or may not be capable

---

[34] See, e.g., *De gen. et corr.* 2.9.335A24-336A12. A discussion of Aristotle's
methodology in this matter may be found in R. McKeon, *op. cit.* (in n. 25
above), pp. 72-74, 113-114.

of integration into a series of literal statements he is making on a given subject,[35] of Plato to mythologize a person or a situation or even a statement in order to find there, through dialectical examination, a glimpse of some universal truth he is seeking. Whether it is a philosopher, a poet, a medical writer or a statesman, Plato's dialectic treats each as someone who may well have uttered a truth but is unaware—or at least not fully aware—of it, and we can be made fully aware of that truth only through the proper kind of dialectical analysis. Plato would not be very happy, I think, to hear that he was being approved for capturing the spirit of some previous thinker. He would not appreciate the zeal with which we impose our standards of history—very narrow ones, he would think—upon him, and he would consider it faint praise indeed that we commend his recreating the spirit of a predecessor when all the time he was bending every effort to employ his own original and hard-won dialectical method to illuminate a truth for us that his source was unable to see.

Though Aristotle does not share Plato's view of the value of myth, nevertheless it is clear that myth does represent a vital tradition for him. The fragments that have survived of his early works, which are generally considered the most Platonic of his writings, do not permit us to judge with any confidence how far the purpose served by myth in these works approaches that of Plato. In the dialogue *Eudemus*, for example, knowledge is claimed for the soul's future life by an argument using the myth of its pre-earthly existence,[36] but the extent to which this procedure may be called "Platonic"—apart from the obvious echoing of Plato's language—is not at all clear. Yet Aristotle's lifelong interest in myth may well be attested for a much later stage of his life, when his activities in teaching and research were over. This is Aristotle toward the close of his days, when, in exile from Athens, no longer surrounded by friends and disciples, and afflicted with the stomach ailment that would shortly cause his death, he wrote, presumably

---

[35] Yet, paradoxically, Aristotle's references to the Pre-Socratics, such as those to the elements of Empedocles mentioned above, have fashioned a myth, and on this myth, interpreted literally, most reconstructions of Pre-Socratic philosophy—even those that assume "distortion" on Aristotle's part—are ultimately based. It is a procedure similar to that of the Christian cosmologists who were led by the *Timaeus* to find Greek notions, such as the elements, in Genesis.

[36] Frag. 41 (Rose, 1886).

in a letter, "The more isolated and solitary I am, the more I have come to love myths." [37]

The myth of the soul's preexistence and fall, which Plato inherits from Empedocles and other predecessors, and transmits to Aristotle in turn, provides a theme that enables us to glance briefly at the way in which the Platonic tradition of myth continues in the later philosophy of the ancient world. Just as many features of the Platonic method, such as his wide-ranging dialectic, are found in Plotinus but altered, particularly in the direction of a lesser flexibility, so his employment of myth is likewise within a narrower range, being centered, like his philosophy as a whole, on the fixed points constituted by the three divine principles, which are for the most part specialized derivations from Platonic texts. The myth of the soul's fall, which is taken from Plato in many of its features, is extended to include the procession of all things from the first principle, with the different levels of causality, which are really distinct from one another not in time or space but in perfection and causal power, being represented as stages of mythical time or points of mythical space. This is especially true of the production of the universe by the creative power of soul. Thus, though rejecting what would seem to him the excessive anthropomorphism inherent in assigning free choice to the first cause of all things, as the Christian doctrine of creation was doing, he indulges in the special kind of anthropomorphism that is associated with his myth. For there was an unquiet faculty of soul, he explains, that was not content with remaining on its lofty level but was desirous of transforming the object of its contemplation into a product that would be completely within its power.[38] This product is the universe, and this stage of the downward process is now so far removed from the original unity that things can no longer hold together but must fall apart into different times and different places.[39]

It is when Plotinus speaks of the individual human soul, however, that the myth of the soul's fall and its need to rise again is especially pervasive. In a scheme in which metaphysical necessity prevails from the highest component to the lowest the soul's responsibility is explained in terms of the myth by which the soul

---

[37] Frag. 668 (ibid.).
[38] Enn. 3.7.11.
[39] Enn. 4.4.15-16.

is attracted to and then immersed in the realm of matter, but with the ability and indeed the obligation to regain its earlier status. The problems involved in the soul's recovery from its fall constitute for Plotinus, as for Plato, the area in which man's moral choice is operative. He follows, he tells us, an ancient teaching to the effect that every virtue, even wisdom itself, is a form of purification.[40] As the soul becomes good and beautiful, and thus achieves a likeness to God, he explains, echoing Plato's *Theaetetus*,[41] it is able to attain a vision of the beautiful, and for this vision we should be prepared to renounce all earthly power and glory.[42] Our fatherland, continues Plotinus, is the place whence we have come, and there our father is also. But to travel to that fatherland we must dispense with our usual means of locomotion, on foot or by carriage or by ship. We must withdraw into ourselves, see where we are lacking in beauty within, and rid ourselves of every imperfection. In this way we become pure vision itself, and this is the only eye that looks upon the real beauty.[43]

The Platonic myth of the soul's fall, usually with Plotinian overtones, is widespread in the later period of ancient philosophy, and it plays an important part in the efforts of the Christian Fathers, especially on the Greek side, to supply a philosophical dimension to the scriptural tradition. One of the outstanding figures who helped to fashion the philosophy of the early Christian era was Gregory of Nyssa, from the century after Plotinus, who, like most of the Greek Fathers of the time, was thoroughly indoctrinated in Greek literature, science and especially philosophy, primarily that of the Platonic tradition. To someone like Gregory the meanings of a scriptural text in all their richness and complexity were by no means immediately evident, and in order to supply them he had to call on whatever resources were available to him, which were largely those offered by his Greek background.

When Gregory, for example, undertakes an interpretation of the opening words of the Lord's Prayer, his efforts to find a significance that goes beyond a simple exhortation to act as sons of a heavenly Father should act lead him to a use of materials that are clearly in the tradition of Plato and Plotinus. Just as in the parable of the

---

[40] *Enn.* 1.6.6.
[41] *Theaet.* 176B.
[42] *Enn.* 1.6.7.
[43] *Enn.* 1.6.9.

prodigal son, he says, the return of the son to his father's house occasions the benevolence of the father, so the words, "Our Father, who art in heaven," when they teach us that the heavenly Father is called upon, remind us of our beloved fatherland and set us on the road leading back to that fatherland. This road is nothing else than a flight from the evils of this earth, and this flight consists in becoming like God, which is to become just and holy and good. The admonition, therefore, to address God as our Father is really a command to become like our heavenly Father through a God-befitting mode of life.[44]

This conclusion of Gregory shows how easy it was for him to interpret a scriptural text as if it belonged naturally to the Greek philosophical tradition, using the flight of the soul from the evils of this earth as it is understood in Plato's *Theaetetus* to mean becoming like God. There is also a suggestion here of the Platonic theory of reminiscence. But, generally speaking, Gregory's point of view is more Plotinian than Platonic, especially in its use of a characteristically Plotinian expression, the return to the lost father-land.

It is interesting to note that before Gregory, Origen, one of the greatest of the Fathers, had interpreted the myth of the soul's fall historically to the extent of holding to a real preexistence of all souls.[45] This doctrine represents a survival of the older Platonic position, with its assimilation of history to myth, which did not generally find a congenial atmosphere in the Christian thinkers, eager as they were to maintain the independence of the newly-fashioned Christian philosophy of history from any view of human life that seemed to them tainted with paganism. For Gregory the fall of the soul is myth, not history; still it serves him not only to interpret a scriptural passage but also, in keeping with its more ancient purpose, to explain the situation of man.

This myth is also found in the Latin world, appearing many times and in many different forms in St. Augustine, for example. In one place he speaks of himself as having been far from God's countenance in the darkness of passion, and this leads him to say, echoing a passage of Plotinus, that it is not by any form of loco-motion that one departs from God or returns to Him. It was not by carriage or ship, not on wing or on foot that the prodigal son went

---

[44] *De oratione dominica* 2 (*PG*, XLIV, 1144B-1145C).
[45] *De principiis* 2.9 (*PG*, XI, 225B-233B; *GCS*, V, 163-172).

to a far-off land to squander what his father had given him on his departure.[46]

Augustine's view of the journey to God, which is sometimes called a return to God, is often expressed in a manner very much like that of Plotinus. Augustine, like Gregory before him, employs the parable of the prodigal son instead of the story of Odysseus, the fabled wanderer of antiquity, found in Plotinus. Augustine sees his own life in terms of the myth of the soul's fall and return, and he identifies himself with the prodigal son, who departed from his fatherland and returned, and likewise with Adam and his fall from grace. This dual identification is basic not only to the structure of the *Confessions* as a philosophical work but also to the understanding that Augustine has of himself as a man representing all men, in whose life we can see all human life.

The role of this myth in his philosophy can be seen also in the ways in which he looks at time. He defines it as a *distentio animi*, a threefold activity by which the mind can extend itself into the future by anticipation and into the past by memory even as it looks at the present.[47] As an activity that belongs to the life of man in a universe of change it is morally neutral. But the soul, from another point of view, finds interests in the universe that distract it from its real purpose for existing, and time can be considered not only a psychological distention but also a moral distraction. As he says in the *Confessions*, "I have fallen apart into times, whose order I do not know, and by turbulent vicissitudes my thoughts are torn asunder, the inmost entrails of my soul." [48] Here is the myth of the soul's fall in a rather Plotinian guise, offering an aspect of time in human life that is not taken account of in the definition of time itself. But Augustine, who makes clear that he has felt the tearing apart of his own soul, is able to instill into the myth a meaning that is distinctively his own.

Augustine was not unaware of the presence of this mythical strain in his thought and he could even be concerned about it. In an early work he speaks of the soul's returning (*rediens*), as it were, to its place of origin, and of its returning (*rediturus*) to heaven.[49] But many years later he says in the *Retractations*

---

[46] *Conf.* 1.18. I have taken up this topic at greater length in *Augustine and the Greek Philosophers* (Villanova, 1967), pp. 47-74.

[47] *Conf.* 11.26.

[48] *Conf.* 11. 29.

[49] *Contra acad.* 2.9.22.

that it would have been safer to speak of going (*iturus*) than of returning to heaven, since in this way he would not have given the impression of accepting the doctrine that the soul, having fallen or being cast down from heaven because of its sins, has been thrust into the body.[50] The discomfort which Augustine felt or had imposed upon him because of the mythical element in his thought is related, it seems to me, to the long-standing controversy about the extent to which he was a Christian or a Neo-Platonist at a given point in his life. Since myth, in Augustine as elsewhere, operates in an entirely different dimension from that of literal language and cannot be systematized with it, much of the controversy is more relevant to the role of myth in Augustine's thought than to the question of his being a Christian or a Neo-Platonist.

This attempt that Augustine makes late in his life to separate the myth of the soul's fall from the main body of his thought, despite its frequent appearance in his works, shows us how far we have come from the employment of this myth in Plato. Not only is there a close relationship in Plato at all times of myth and history to each other and to his dialectical method, but in the higher reaches of his thought dialectic, myth and history are identical. This identity, which is explicitly denied in Aristotle on the basis of what he conceives to be the proper methodology, becomes looser even within the Platonic tradition, as in Plotinus, despite all efforts, apparent or real, to be faithful to the master. Christian Platonism, in particular, was obliged to offer a philosophy of history that was in accord with the doctrine of salvation, a philosophy that explained the course of time by means of points, fixed and non-repeating, namely, the creation of man along with a universe to serve his needs, the Incarnation of God among men, and the eventual consummation of the universe when it will serve no further purpose. In Augustine the breaking up of the Platonic identity of dialectic, myth and history—or what is left of it—is very clearly observed, and no Platonist has come along since him to restore it.

We are the true heirs of Plato, despite the lapse of the centuries. The Platonism we have inherited, however, is not one that we have taken directly from his hand but rather one that has been passed on to us by many intervening generations, each of which has modified it, deliberately or otherwise, in accordance with its

---

[50] *Retract.* 1.1.3.

own needs and understanding. The peculiar unity that characterized his thought has been broken, by time itself, we might say, into its various components, somewhat as white light—to use a perhaps fanciful analogy—is separated into many colored lights by a prism. The problem of bringing these colored lights back to their single source is like the one we face in regaining the lost unity of Plato, and it is this problem more than any other that gives rise to the difficulties and controversies to be found in Platonic scholarship. I believe that the unity of dialectic, myth and history constitutes the very core of Plato's philosophy, and I would like to hope that, for our benefit, and not just in the field of scholarship, this single, simple vision of his may some day be restored.

# PLATO AND SCIENCE

## FRIEDRICH SOLMSEN

Plato's science is the work of his old age. It surely is a matter for amazement that Plato whose first philosophic concern had been questions of ethics and citizenship and who had gradually moved on to metaphysics and epistemology, should late in life come forward with a large scale account of Nature, an account whose influence on later ages is matched by the work of very few scientists, and certainly no outsider.[1] Why should the physical world have become for him a subject of such painstaking and penetrating study? Why should he year after year endeavor to understand objects and phenomena that he had formerly declared unsatisfactory material for investigation and devoid of interest for man? Quite probably he had considered them inferior.[2] As long as man's excellences and the right treatment of soul were in the center of his interest, he was dealing with human values. The highest value toward which all others point was what the Greeks called "the good." In Nature good and value had no place. Also moral virtues, such as justice, and whatever else qualified for a philosopher's attention had to be something permanent, basically unchanging, so that we may grasp its essence—no easy task, to be sure, never accomplished, yet for ever to be pursued—whereas Nature was a realm of change, growth, and decrease, where things arose and passed away, and where nothing remained stable—or remained at all.

---

[1] Paul Shorey in a brilliant essay: "Plato and the History of Science" (*Proc. Am. Philos. Soc.* 66, 1927, 161 ff.) discusses Plato himself, scholarly and scientific interpretations of Plato, and modern science with never faltering magisterial confidence; stripping Plato of everything that is religious, mythical or imaginative—mere ornaments or concessions to the taste and convention of his time—he leaves us with a thinker who is nothing if not a scientist, ahead of his own day and of ours (or at least of Shorey's). I have not set my sights so high. With G. E. R. Lloyd, "Plato as a natural scientist" (*J. Hell. Stud.* 88 (1968) 78 ff.) I am in agreement on major questions. My debt to F. M. Cornford's masterpiece, *Plato's Cosmology* (Cambridge, 1937) is far greater than my references—simply to his name—indicate.

[2] The most noteworthy statement of dissatisfaction occurs in the *Phaedo* (96A-99E). See further *Philebus* 58E ff.

•

Plato had other reasons for his lack of confidence and genuine interest. Why then would he go at all, and why would he in the dialogue *Timaeus* go so profoundly into matters that to all appearance were not germane to his philosophy? A part of the answer is that mathematics helped him to find his way. Mathematics had for some time enjoyed Plato's esteem. In essential aspects its study was akin to the new subject that he himself tried to build up in the area of the human good and the norms of our action. As he saw it, the mathematician, even if he drew circles, diagonals, triangles and other figures in the sand, was not actually investigating the properties of these particular visible objects; his theorems were valid for the circle as such, the triangle as such. This suggested another, higher level of reality. The discoveries and the theorems remained, even when the figure in the sand had disappeared. This corresponded to Plato's convictions about true justice, true courage, and the other true and truly real norms and exemplary Forms that had to be stable and permanent, exempt from all fluctuation, and also perfect. By their perfection they contrast with what men know and call by the same names—justice, courage etc.—and what they practice very imperfectly, if at all—for often enough they do not even try to practice them. These true virtues as permanent and ideal Forms belong like all other Platonic Forms and like the mathematical entities to a different order of being.

Still despite such agreement in essentials, Plato found much to criticize in the mathematics of his day. In Book VII of the *Republic* he pointed out the large discrepancy between mathematics as it was and as it ought to be. And he initiated a reform. This would not be admitted by everybody; but mathematics as we find it in the *Elements* of Euclid two generations later shows us the subject organized as Plato desired.[3] This reorganization of mathematics, in which Plato is likely to have enjoyed the collaboration of Eudoxus and other great mathematicians in the Academy (his school),

---

[3] Appreciation and criticism of mathematics are combined in *Resp.* VI 510D-511E; VII 522C-531D (esp. 525B f.). Eva Sachs (*Die fünf Platonischen Körper*, Berlin, 1917) was the first to establish valid relations between Plato and the development of mathematics at his time. For a recent treatment see K. von Fritz, *Grundprobleme der Geschichte der ant. Wissenschaft* (Berlin-New York, 1971) 250 ff., 335 ff. with my review *Am. Journ. of Philol.* 95 (1974), 341 ff.; see also "Platos Einfluss auf die Bildung der mathemat. Methode" in Konrad Gaiser, (ed.), *Das Platonbild* (Hildesheim, 1969) 125 ff., a paper of 1931 reprinted because of the questions raised rather than for the theories advanced in it.

may be considered a prior condition to his thoroughgoing reform
of physics.

What Plato did for mathematics may be illustrated by a few
examples. Plato criticized mathematics as he found it on the
ground that its practicioners could not render account of what
they did. They did not even "know" (in true, Platonic knowledge)
their starting points and concepts. The obvious way of rendering
account of something is to define it; and in Euclid you find at the
opening of each Book of the *Elements* a series of definitions, e.g.:
"a point is that which has no parts"; "an obtuse angle is an angle
greater than a right angle". These definitions serve as basis for the
more complex definitions, in Euclid, and for the further proceedings,
especially the demonstrations. My second example is Plato's
insistence that a student of mathematics should realize what all
branches of this subject have in common.[4] An organ for grasping
what is common to all instances of a virtue, of justice, of courage
and so forth, is essential for the philosopher or dialectician as he
moves upward to the Platonic Forms. He must distill the "one in
many," the character common and essential for all physical realiza-
tions of a Form. In mathematics the items common to all branches
are the so-called axioms. "If equals are added to equals, the wholes
are equals" is as true in arithmetic as it is in geometry or in
astronomy. So is "if two items are equal to a third, they are equal
to one another." Actually we have information about other progress
in the direction of what is common; but it would take us too far
afield.

Allow me instead to mention an innovation of a somewhat
different type. I spoke of the branches of mathematics. In his
*Republic* when Plato dwells on the educational value of each and
passes from one branch to the next, he notices a gap in the sequence:
arithmetic, geometry, astronomy, harmonics. There ought to be a
subject between geometry, which is the study of two-dimensional
figures, and astronomy which deals with bodies, i.e. tri-dimensional
objects *in motion*. The study of tri-dimensional objects as such,
if so far neglected, should surely be taken up. We know this subject

---

[4] *Resp.* VII 531C9-D4; cf. Cornford "Mathematics and Dialectic in the
*Republic* VI and VII" reprinted from *Mind* 41 (1932) 37-52, 173-190 in
R. E. Allen (ed.), *Studies in Plato's Metaphysics* (London, 1965) 61 ff.,
esp. 82 ff. My own opinion—compatible with Cornford's—is set forth in
*Kleine Schriften* (Hildesheim, 1968) I 316 ff.

as solid geometry or stereometry. Probably brilliant mathematicians had just begun to open this field when Plato called for its cultivation. Long before he died the fundamental constructions were achieved by a close friend of his, Theaetetus, another mathematician of the Academy, and we shall see what ingenious use Plato makes of them for the foundations of a new physics.[5]

I am however not suggesting that Plato's friendly attitude to mathematics, even if it increased with the reforms, is the sole cause for his intense occupation with physics late in his life. Organic developments of his own thought led in the same direction. Once his doctrine of eternal, unchanging Forms had been built up, he could from this position take a more sympathetic attitude to large realms he had previously disregarded or dismissed. The Forms, as I had to emphasize, are stable and at rest. But besides what is at rest, it is necessary to recognize also a world of motion and change. In one of his later dialogues, the *Sophist*, Plato has reached this point. ". . . it seems that only one course is open to the philosopher who values knowledge and understanding above all else. . . He must declare that Reality or the sum of things is both at once, all that is unchangeable and all that is in change,"[6] a decision and declaration of the greatest consequence; for it sanctions a philosophical treatment of physics—and of physics in its broadest, most comprehensive form.

Still, despite such hopeful developments, when Plato in the *Timaeus* comes forward with his new scheme of physical science, he presents it in the form of a myth. And myth, though Plato often resorts to it, never ranks for him on a par with dialectic, the germane philosophical way toward true knowledge. A myth may embody beliefs and convictions that logical discourse could not establish; but the content of a myth is always something that *may* be, that is not too far from the truth. It is, as Plato himself says in the *Timaeus*, a collection of "likely tales."[7] To a higher status physical science cannot aspire, and reluctant though we may be, we have to accept this marriage of myth and science as reflecting Plato's reservations about the truth value of physics.

---

[5] For solid geometry see *Resp.* VII 531C9-D4. Cf. again Eva Sachs, *op. cit.* (n. 3), esp. 88 ff. as well as Paul Friedländer, *Plato. An Introduction* (engl. trlt., New York, 1958) ch. 14.

[6] *Soph.* 249C10 ff.

[7] *Tim.* 29B-D; 48C f.; 59C f.; 68D. From this point references in the notes are to the *Timaeus* unless another work is indicated.

On the other hand, the mythical form made it legitimate to incorporate in this account besides scientific doctrine a good deal that we would not expect in a scientific treatise. There are references to reincarnation. There is a creator god, whom we best take as a mythical symbol and appreciate as a most useful device, but he surely is not the last word of either Plato's science or his religion. There is furthermore in the *Timaeus* a most profound disquisition about the nature of space, metaphysical rather than physical in tenor, and there is a world soul, a very strange conception for us, and it would appear even stranger if I were to describe its structure to you in detail.[8] By means of it Plato makes his Cosmos a living entity; but it is pivotal also for his astronomy and contributes greatly to the perfection of his Cosmos. But why should the Cosmos be perfect, in what sense is it perfect and what does this idea entail?

Here you must allow me one more word about the large realm of change, process, and motion, which we saw, Plato had decided to rehabilitate and for which his general denominator is "movement," local motion being for him the prototype of changes. Movement, as I have kept repeating, contrasts with Rest, and to the eternal Forms that are at rest and unchanging, Plato several times applies a description, which has almost become a formula. They are "persisting always in the same manner alike" (ἀεὶ κατὰ τὰ αὐτὰ ὡσαύτως).. Thus we may imagine the dramatic impact of the discovery that there were also movements to which this description applied and—that these movements were right here in our visible, physical world. These movements that "persisted always in the same manner alike" were the revolutions of the planets. To the Greeks the very word "planet" had suggested that they drifted about, following no regular path. "Erring body" is what it means. Yet during Plato's life-time long term records kept in Egypt and Babylonia became known and showed that these bodies followed a recognizable path and in identical time periods returned to the same place.[9] It was probably Plato's friends and fellow workers in

---

[8] Creator: 28A ff., 29D ff. (I do not refer to the subsidiary creator gods introduced 42D nor shall I deal with the opposition and cooperation between Reason and Necessity; see on this topic Cornford 159 ff. most of whose explanations are still valid). Space: 48E-53C. World Soul: 34B-37C and *pass.*

[9] See esp. *Legg.* VII 821c-822c (also "Plato," *Epin.* 986a-987e). Regularity of the movements is implied at *Tim.* 39C5 ff. For Egyptian and Babylonian records see Arist. *DeCaelo* II 12, 292A7 ff.

the Academy who by this revolutionary discovery changed the world picture completely. For the entire celestial region extending from the outermost Heaven of the fixed stars to the sphere of the moon was henceforth a theatre of awe-inspiring regularity and of an order so brilliantly devised by a divine Mind and so sublime that it called not only for admiration but for worship. When the mathematicians or astronomers were able to explain these periodic revolutions of the planets as circular movements, the perfection of this higher world was sealed; [10] for circle, sphere, and globe, whose circumference is equidistant everywhere from the center, were for the Greeks the most beautiful figures. A result of this great cosmological revolution was that for roughly 2,000 years until the days of Newton the physical world consisted of two completely distinct parts. Henceforth celestial physics investigated laws and studied movements intricate, yet surpassingly beautiful, whereas the other part of physics was far less august and had to deal with the troublesome, not nearly so predictable processes on our Earth. Whether this dichotomy, for which Plato bears a large responsibility [11] was for good or ill we may consider later. One thing is certain; you will readily imagine how welcome this superior dignity of the celestial region was to mediaeval thinkers, Christian and others. "The heavens declare the glory of God." Surely they do, if even pagans bear witness.

This pattern of regular movements bestows unique worth primarily on the celestial area, but beyond it on the Cosmos as a whole. Plato's Cosmos is the alpha and omega of his physical system, the frame within which every problem of science must be treated. Such had never yet been its position. Quite to the contrary, two centuries before the *Timaeus*, when physical speculation began in Greece, it opened wider vistas. The first great cosmologist, Anaximander, posited an all-encompassing Infinite, formless itself; yet from it there would from time to time break off huge chunks that gradually took shape and eventually the shape of a world. But this world would pass away again; and innumerable other

---

10 Arist. , *Metaph.* Lambda 8. Cf. Jaeger, *Aristotle. Fundamentals of the History of his Development* (Engl. trlt., 2nd ed., Oxford, 1948) 342 ff.; D. R. Dicks, *Early Greek Astronomy to Aristotle* (Ithaca, N. Y., 1970) 151 ff., esp. 175 (also 108 and *pass.*).

11 See again Jaeger, *op. cit.* 140 ff., 164 ff., 383, 389 f.; also for the cosmological dichotomy in mediaeval thought and its ancient basis C. S. Lewis, *The Discarded Image* (Cambridge, 1964) 3 f., 32, 92 ff., 120 f.

worlds would arise, grow, decrease, and disintegrate—it is not quite clear whether successively or even simultaneously. Between Anaximander and Plato further cosmological systems had been advanced, highly original, ever more different from Anaximander's. Yet Plato's exaltation of the Cosmos and its perfect form is the complete reversal of the traditional scheme with its amorphous Infinite.[12] Again you may ask whether Plato by excluding Infinity, by excluding an unlimited Universe and allowing one world, one Cosmos only, was not guilty of a retrograde step, fatal from the view-point of contemporary astronomy and that of the last two centuries, though not of five ancient centuries nor of ten mediaeval. This, I assure you, is the last time that I raise this disturbing question before I try to answer it at the end. Now let us rather hear how Plato himself justifies his one and only Cosmos:

"Let us state for what reason becoming and the sum of things were framed by him who framed them. He (*scil.* the creator god) was good, and in the good no jealousy of anything can ever arise. So being without jealousy, he wished everything to become as much as possible like himself. Desiring then that all things should be good and as far as possible nothing in a bad condition, the Creator took over all that was visible and not at rest but in discordant and unordered motion and brought it from disorder into order; for he judged order to be in every way better than disorder." [13] You may now understand why this science is cast in the form of a myth. But may I ask you to note also the occurrence of the words "good" and "better" in these sentences. For, as I mentioned, the physical world had originally been of small interest to Plato because he saw no "good" realized in it.[14] Here he introduces it by means of order (τάξις). We shall later come to know two other manifestations of the "good" that supplement order down here where its sway is weaker. Moreover Plato's creator endows the

---

[12] For pre-Platonic cosmology cf. Charles H. Kahn, *Anaximander and the Origins of Greek Cosmology* (New York, 1960), an illuminating book, where however the topics most closely investigated are apt to prevent rather than to facilitate a recognition of the Platonic revolution; on this point see the brief but excellent comments in Cornford 52. In Plato's scheme the shapeless, indefinite matrix survives as the Receptacle, "mother and nurse of all genesis" which cannot however produce without being activated by the Forms.

[13] 29D6-30A6.

[14] See again *Phaedo* 97B8 ff. An emphatic assertion of cosmic order in an early dialogue (*Gorg.* 507E6 ff.) should not remain unmentioned.

entire Cosmos with those qualities that for some time—ever since
Parmenides—had been standard requirements for perfect being.
It is unique as the one and only Cosmos in existence, is compact,
is complete in that it contains the total amount of the four elements; also being a globe it has the best of all shapes, and it is
self-sufficient, balanced, firmly structured.[15] One predicate is
missing: eternity or immortality. For the Cosmos has been created
and has a beginning. However, as interpreters ancient and modern
again and again try to discount the creation as purely mythical,
metaphorical or methodical, we may add that the Cosmos has a
body and is visible as well as tangible, reasons enough to exclude
immortality, which pertains to the Platonic Forms that are grasped
not by the eyes but by pure thought. In the world of the senses this
Cosmos may be the most beautiful thing; [16] yet like all physical
objects it must have a model in the realm of Forms, an eternal
Cosmos to be contemplated by the mind. Eternity is the principal
difference between the model and the copy. Plato has often in his
dialogues spoken of the Forms as imperishable, without origin
and without end. All of this implies eternity; but only here in the
context of the *Timaeus* does Plato come forward with a concept
and word for eternity and proceeds to define the meaning. The
definition avails itself of the contrast between the ideal world and
this physical. The latter as a copy of the eternal embodies in its
structure a copy of eternity. This copy is Time.

Plato's definitions of eternity, of time and of their mutual
relation are epoch-making. I quote and interpolate comments:

---

[15] For these and other Parmenidean (or Eleatic) motifs in *Tim.* 30C-34B
see besides Cornford 53 ff., W. K. C. Gurthrie, *A History of Greek Philosophy*
II (Cambr., 1965), 47 f.

[16] 29A5. For a recent statement of the case for an eternal Cosmos see
Leonardo Tarán, in *Essays in Ancient Greek Philosophy*, edited by John
P. Anton with George L. Kustas (Albany, New York, 1971) 372 ff. Scholars
who insist that the creation in the *Timaeus* is a myth usually fail to consider
how likely Plato was to treat physics and cosmology in any other medium.
Plato's own remarks (see above n. 7) do not encourage this idea.—That the
myth of the *Timaeus* is *sui generis* is true, but a myth it remains. For a
firmly reasoned defense of the creation motif see Vlastos in R. E. Allen
(above n. 4) 379 ff., 401 ff. I do not suggest a literal acceptance of "creation"
as such or of details in the account. Rather my point would be that Plato
regardless of preference and praise by which he sets the Cosmos apart
from all other physical entities (33 A1 ff., 37C ff., 38B7, 41A7 ff.), yet
keeps it definitely in the realm of becoming, movement, and change.

"Of eternity abiding in one"—meaning: for ever in the same condition, yet "one" is essential—"(the Creator) makes an image partaking of eternity, moving by numbers, which we call Time." Numbers are somehow derivative of "one". "Moving" may suggest a shortcoming rather than an imitation of "abiding"; yet "moving by numbers" conveys the idea of a regular repetition, one by one, and thus qualifies as image of "abiding in one." Once more, then, with slight variations: "Of eternity abiding in one, the image Time partakes, moving by numbers." Numbers articulate, and if Plato thinks of the steady movements in Heaven as Time, this definition of Time need not strike you as mysterious; for relying on the "moving by numbers" of Sun, moon and the starry Heaven we all count years, months, days, hours, minutes, seconds, going much farther than Plato's contemporaries were equipped to do.

I wished I could dwell on the momentous significance of this Platonic definition; in the first place to point out how new a departure and how truly Platonic definition as such is (even if we do not speak of its use here as a vehicle of deep metaphysical thought); next to remind you of quite different conceptions of Time that had been current in Greece: Time the healer of wounds, Time the great teacher, Time the judge even if generations have to go by before the sins of the fathers are visited on the children. Time ὁ πανδαμάτωρ is a great conqueror and destroyer, and Time, as Sophocles says, brings everything to light and hides it again.[17] Plato ignores these and other aspects of Time to select the one which furnishes structure. The influence of the definition extends very far. St. Augustine for one agrees that Time and this world came simultaneously into existence. Throughout the Middle Ages the opposition of eternity and time remained alive and fundamental. Late in the Middle Ages time as measurement for motion comes back to have its own career. You know the 't' factor (= *tempus*, time) in the "law of fall" and in Newton's definition of Force; in fact, I understand—or rather I gather, for please do not for a moment believe I understand—that Einstein's celebrated definition

---

[17] Soph. *Aj.* 646 ff.; see also e.g. Solon 36.3 West; Pindar *Ol.* 2.16 f., 10.55; Simon. 26.5 Page. Aristotle lists functions and effects commonly associated with time in *Phys.* IV 10; 12.221A28 ff.; 13.222B16 ff. Particularly illuminating studies are Hermann Fränkel, "Die Zeitauffassung in der frühgriech. Literatur" (*Wege und Formen frühgriech. Denkens*, Munich, 1960, 1 ff.) and J. de Romilly. *Time in Greek Tragedy* (Ithaca, N.Y., 1968).

of energy, by including the speed of light, once more gives Time its due.[18]

In Plato's Cosmos too light functions as a measure, although not by its speed. Referring to the Sun, he calls it "the light which the Creator kindled. . . so that there might be a brightly visible measure for comparing speed and slowness of the heavenly revolutions. Thanks to it we are aware of the sequence of day and night, realize the completion of a year when the Sun has gone through its own circle, and become familiar with number and counting that are no small help toward philosophy, most precious gift of God to man." Dante is speaking in a very Platonic vein when in "Paradiso" he calls the Sun "the greatest of the ministers of Nature" ("ministro maggior della Natura") "who with his light measures Time" ("col suo lume il tempo ne misura") and "communicates the good by which the world above turns the world below". Here "the good above" may mean the divine good, the heavenly order, or the cycle of the seasons which causes the annual growth and life here below; it may relate to still other providential concerns and influences from above; yet whichever way we take it, the passage is, like so many others in Dante inspired by the Platonic—Aristotelian world view. [19]

So far "order" has for us been the manifestation of the good. But Plato's "good" has two other ways of entering the visible world. One of them is form, the other is purpose. Form dominates Plato's explanation of physical objects, their actions and interactions. Every object in the sublunary world is for him either an element or a mixture of elements. As elements he recognizes fire, water, air and earth, the four that about a hundred years before his days Empedocles had made the constituents of bodies. But

---

[18] For St. Augustine cf. *de civ. Dei* XI (esp. chapters 4 and 6) where in true Platonic style the beginning of time and of the world coincide and where the opposition between time and eternity is treated in the framework of the large Platonic dichotomy between the spiritual and the visible. (St. Augustine's psychological approach to time, discussed by John F. Callahan above, p. 83, is a different, though of course not unrelated subject).

[19] *Paradiso* 10.28-30; cf. 9.107 f. Generally speaking, Dante is closer to the Aristotelian-Ptolemaic tradition. Regarding the thoughts embodied in these passages Plato and Aristotle are in basic agreement, though the latter knows no realm of transcendent entities (like the eternal model of our Cosmos in the *Timaeus*) and eternity figures in his scheme not as model and contrast of time but "embraces the whole of time and infinity" (= time in its infinite extension, *de caelo* I 9, 279A25 ff.).

when Plato gives each of these elements an atomic structure, he
parts company with Empedocles and moves closer to another
school of early physicists, the so-called atomists (whose chief
representative is Democritus), and when after combining these two
conceptions, elements and atoms, he still provides the atoms of
all four elements with "most beautiful" mathematical "shape,"
he embarks on a completely new departure. Here he is once more
opening the door for mathematics, and indeed for that new branch
of mathematics that he himself had postulated and encouraged,
solid geometry. For these "most beautiful forms" are the regular
solid bodies that had been quite recently constructed by his friend
and associate, the mathematician Theaetetus.[20] To the element
earth Plato assigns the cube with its six equal surfaces, to fire the
pyramid with four such surrounding planes; the water atom is a
body of twenty equal surfaces, the so called icosahedron, and the
atom of air with eight such faces goes by the name of octahedron.

It is convenient to refer to these regular solid bodies as atoms,
but we do so at our peril. For in Plato's scheme they do not behave
as atoms should. They break up, and not simply into their surfaces
but into particular kinds of triangles that compose these surfaces.
And again as in the case of the regular solid bodies themselves,
Plato is emphatic on the superlative beauty or elegance of these
triangles. A welcome assurance if we consider how much he con-
structs with their help. For the same kind of triangles that form
sides of the pyramid also compose the surfaces of the octahedron,
the air-atom and again the twenty sides encompassing the water
atom. Yet for each of these two a larger number of triangles is
needed. Fortunately I can spare you most of the arithmetic. One
example will suffice. When water is overcome by fire, the process
which is normally called boiling, this would in Plato's scheme be a
breaking-up of water atoms, those bodies with twenty surfaces,
each of which consists of six triangles. The breaking-up sets free
twenty times six, i.e. 120 triangles—and they recompose in this
instance into two atoms of air. Atoms of air, as I said, have eight
surfaces, again each built up of six triangles. This sums up to
forty-eight, and if the one hundred and twenty triangles of one
water atom now reorganize as air atoms, two of these air atoms
would only absorb twice 48 = 96 triangles, and 24 would remain,

---

[20] 53C4-55C6. Cf. again Eva Sachs and Paul Friedländer as cited above
(n. 3 and n. 5 respectively).

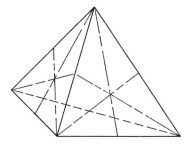

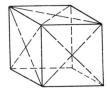

The Atom of Fire                    The Atom of Earth

From Paul Friedländer, *Plato: An Introduction* (Princeton, 1969, second edition) Figures 1 and 2 (after p. 256).

just enough to form a pyramid which needs six triangles for each of its four sides. The upshot is that one water atom in the process of boiling turns into two of air and one of fire, the fire probably being meant to account for the hot quality of the steam.[21] From the equation of one unit of water with two of air and one of fire it surely is a far cry to the familiar chemical formula, which defines water as $H_2O$; but for some advance in this direction, for some use of ratios and of mathematics in his approach to such substances Plato should be given credit. Once this is granted, I am the last to minimize the difference of hydrogen and oxygen from fire and air or see much in common between Plato's mathematical construction from a-priori premises and a chemical analysis.

As historians we had better compare Plato with his precursors and admit that he has succeeded in overcoming a stumbling block; for some of them, as for instance Empedocles with his never changing four elements, had been unable to account for their mutual transformation. Plato, having chosen the regular mathematical bodies as his physical principles, must justify his choice by showing that he can explain as much or more than any of the earlier physicists could on the basis of his principles (Empedocles by his four elements, Democritus by his non-mathematical atoms). Still this competitive motive, while surely present, should not blind us to his genuine desire to understand the substance of the largest possible number of physical objects. Every object in the sublunary world that is not an element is a mixture of elements; and it is as mixtures, or at the most as mixtures with a few additional specifications and refinements that Plato defines items

---

[21] Cf. 56C8-57C6: for boiling see 56D6-8.

as diverse as rock and oil, gold and wine, yet also processes such as the formation of snow or fog, of melting, freezing; and there are large sections packed with details about still other physical, chemical and indeed also psychological subjects that I must leave untouched.[22]

However, tying up with what I have said and bearing in mind how essential Form is in Plato's thought, I wish to clarify two general aspects of his construction. The triangles of which you have heard and the regular solid bodies furnish him with solutions for all problems of transformation, interaction, and composition. If a physical body is mixed of earth and water, cubes and icosahedra are there to build it. Plato has no need for any complementary factor to cooperate with these formative and architectonic principles; in particular he has no need for matter. What he does need to assure subsistence for his elements and compounds is space. Each object must besides its structure also have a place where it comes into being. Thus we understand that Plato does not, like Aristotle, require a concept of matter to permit the realization of a Form, but instead pairs Space with Form. In a passage which epitomizes a profound metaphysical train of thought he likens the Form to the father, space which receives the Form to the mother, that which arises through their joint action to the offspring.[23]

Now that we have moved down to the actual physical product, let us turn back again and move upward. If elements are built from their atoms and atoms have the shape of regular solid bodies, we have clearly passed from physics into mathematics; and if solid bodies are composed out of their surfaces and these taken apart into triangles, we have left the realm of three dimensions. Furthermore, if the sides of these triangles have ratios like $1:1$ or $1:2$, we have risen not only above the corporeal but even above the two-dimensional. We have left the concrete beneath us; we are dealing with non-physical, perhaps I might say, abstract entities.

---

[22] 58C5-61C2.

[23] 50D2. To the question which I admit suggests itself and which has often been raised, *scil.* whether the solid bodies are "filled" Plato provides no answer. More precisely, he shows no awareness of this question, and I should be content to think that preoccupied as he was with the form and derivation of these bodies, their "content" never acquired importance for him. The question may well be misconceived and not germane to his approach. To leave these bodies "empty" is, I admit, awkward, but it surely is no less awkward to saddle Plato with doctrines of which his account contains no hint. For an ingenious suggestion see Cornford 181 ff., 229.

Higher and higher turns our road; exactly how high Plato does not reveal. For at the point where he might have done so, he hides behind the mysterious words: "The principles still higher than these God knows and of men whoever is dear to him." [24] In this select company one would like to be included; but having received no sign that I am among the elect, I may as well refrain from speculation [25] and turn to purpose, the third way in which the good manifests itself in Nature.

To illustrate purpose, we must consider man, by all odds the most precious creation in this imperfect sublunary world. In the physiology of man purpose is present on every level of composition. What are these levels? [26] Man, being like everything else in this world put together of the four elements, the first order of composition would be the tissues; bone, flesh, blood, sinew etc., which at the time were considered homogeneous and undifferentiated and had even before Plato been explained as mixtures of earth, water, air and fire. On the next level above them the organs have their place, composed of the tissues and showing far more differentiation in their structure. The lung for instance is described as "perforated within by cavities like a sponge" and "being reached by the channels of the windpipe"; [27] thus it must be considerably more complex than a tissue. The highest level above tissues and organs is occupied by the integrated organism where the Creator's providence has with great circumspection given tissues and organs their best possible place, shape and function. Thanks to the Creator motif Plato's account is probably the *first* integrated physiology of

---

[24] 53D6 f.

[25] Interpreters tend to understand the reference "upward" as pointing to numbers, especially to "the One" which in the thought of the late Plato and in his so called "oral doctrine" occupied a place of great importance as the principle (*arche*) from which numbers and, directly or indirectly, much else was derived. Great effort and ingenuity have gone into the reconstruction of this doctrine which need not have replaced the theory of Forms but may as well have been intended to supplement or support it. Most of the details are obscure. The group of determined German scholars (J. H. Krämer, K. Gaiser and others) who have been for some time engaged in the reconstruction of this doctrine has lately acquired an ally in the American philosopher J. N. Findlay (*Plato, the Written and Unwritten Doctrines*, 1974).— Krämer's basic work is *Arete bei Plato und Aristoteles* (*Abhandlg. Heidelb. Akad.*, 1959, 6); for a recent bibliography of the enterprise see Heinz Happ, *Hyle* (Berlin-New York, 1971) 816 ff., esp. s.v. Krämer.

[26] For the "levels," a doctrine embryonic in Plato, fully developed in Aristotle, see 82B8.

[27] 70C1 ff.

man. Contemporary schools of physicians are imperfectly known
but can hardly have had anything comparable.

I ought to discuss tissues first and proceed from them to organs;
but Plato himself begins with the organs and I find it convenient
to follow his example. To realize how completely purpose dominates
Plato's treatment of the organs, we must remember that for Plato
man has not only a body but also a soul. The body must serve the
nobler purposes of soul, even though what is good for the soul may
not always be good for the body. A longer life, for instance
could have been secured in Plato's view if man's head had been
protected by a larger application of flesh and sinews; but the
heavy weight of more flesh would have dulled the functioning of the
brain, and thus the life, though longer, would have been of inferior
quality [28] intellectually.

Soul for Plato was not a biological but an ethical conception. In
ethics it had acquired organs of its own, but not physiological.
More commonly they are known as "parts of soul." They are
the ruling part, which is mind, a second translated best as "spirited
impulse", and the third finally represents desires and appetites.
As Plato provides for each of these parts a home in the body,
you may expect a very humanistic physiology.

First of all mind, the best and in fact divine part of soul, receives
its habitation in the head, where it is in a position of command and
control. By means of the neck it is separated from the other parts, of
which the spirited impulse is settled in the heart, while the desires
for food and drink are housed still lower, in the belly, and again
separated by the midriff.[29]

Plato defines the role of the heart as the "knot of blood-vessels
and the fountain of the blood which moves vigorously around all
the limbs." Thus we are safely on scientific ground; yet when we
learn what purpose the heart serves we are in the midst of ethics.
The spirited part which is here located is relatively close to the
seat of reason in the head, so that when its own vigor is aroused in
say, anger or indignation, it may receive a word of command from
reason, calm down and spread peace through all that is aroused
in the body. Still, as it may beat fast and throb impatiently, the
lung has been placed near it, soft and yielding by nature, and
thanks to its respiratory function able to cool the heart and quiet

[28]  75A7-C7.
[29]  69D6 ff.; (cf. 44D2 ff.)

it.[30] The heat in the heart incidentally is due to the element fire, whereas the lung receives both air and water, the cooler elements.

If this doctrine leaves you amazed and aghast, you may learn with interest how two eminent Greek biologists, Aristotle and Galen, later used and modified the Platonic purposes. Aristotle has banished ethics from physiology. Also writing not a myth but a sternly scientific treatise, he refuses to give mind a physical basis and allows only one purpose for the relatively useless brain. Being cold, dry, insensitive to touch and, as far as he knew, unconnected with any sense organs, it serves by its coolness to counterbalance the heat of the body's central area; and when it sends down coolness in large portions it induces sleep. The lung surely is the organ of breathing; its sponginess opens wide for this process. But the theory that the lung is a cushion for the throbbing of the heart must be abandoned. For such throbbing is confined to man, who alone has hope and expectation. Moreover in most animals the distance of the lung from the heart is too large to allow assistance.[31] You know the theory against which Aristotle is polemizing and realize the difference made by the use of comparative anatomy. For the brain of course a position has been abandoned, which Galen and even others before him recovered. In Galen the brain is definitely the seat of intelligence and the center to which all sense functions report. The heart "is as it were the hearthstone and source of innate heat by which the animal is governed," and again "the heart seems to supply the lung with nutriment from the blood and do the lung this service in return for the air which the heart receives from it".[32] Strange or familiar as individual doctrines may sound to you, it is obvious that moral purpose has given way to physiological function. Effective operation of the body, not the good of the soul has become the controlling idea. Even so the great Platonic architect and planner is still felt in the background, also with Galen.

We postponed a look at Plato's treatment of the tissues. Ancient physiologists, including the philosophers, differ a good deal as to the basic or the most vital tissue. The blood had once been raised

---

[30] 69E3-70D6.

[31] See Arist. de part. anim. II 7; 10, 656A14 ff. (brain); III 6, 668B33 ff., esp. 669A14 ff. (lung).

[32] de usu partium VI 2 (I 301.3 ff. Helmreich); 7 (I 315 ff. H.); 10 (I 324.16 ff. H.). Cf. Galen On the Usefulness of parts. . . translated by Margaret Tallmadge May (Ithaca, N.Y., 1968) I 279 f., 292, 296.

to this place of honor; for Aristotle the bony frame is the scaffolding of the body to which flesh and everything else has been attached.[33] Plato too assures us that the bones have been fashioned with great care, yet not for their own sake, but because they enclose something of far greater worth, the marrow. For marrow is most truly the stuff of life, where soul is tied to body. Of all four elements the smoothest and at the same time firmest triangles were used in its composition. The word for marrow had in early Greek poetry also stood for "life"; yet Plato has reasons of his own for giving it such an exalted status.[34] For the marrow is in substance identical with the seed or life-giving sperm, yet also with the brain, the domicile of mind and reason. Survival or what the *Symposium* calls immortality through progeny is entrusted to its keeping, yet it also provides the substratum for the immortality of soul. Of all living beings man alone stands upright with his head turned heavenward, his skull imitating the shape of the heavenly vault. Thus the movements of his mind should orient themselves by the unbroken rhythm of the celestial revolutions, be in tune with the cosmic regularity and harmony. Keeping free of all disturbance from without, the best part of the soul may remain untainted in its original divine condition and, as Plato elsewhere in the myth indicates, return after death to its heavenly abode in the star allotted to it.

Surely this is not what we to-day call science. Far too much ethics intrudes, and far too much metaphysics. Plato knows life and the world as they are but he knows too much else. Even if we now leave the creator god on one side, the rule of soul in the Cosmos and the dominant position of soul in man's physiology must cause serious misgivings to anyone brought up on modern science. True, the physiology of this dialogue includes chapters on deficiencies, where Plato examines also deficiencies and illnesses of soul and discusses troubles arising between body and soul, especially if they are ill-matched. He is without doubt the discoverer of psychosomatic interactions,[35] a great achievement, but for stern judges it

---

[33] See Empedocles A 78; 86.11; B 98 Diels-Kranz (blood); Arist., *de part. anim.* II 9, 654B29 ff. (bones).

[34] 73B-D. For what follows cf. also 91A4 ff.; 44D; 43C-44C.

[35] 86A-88E (or 89D); note esp. 87D1-88D, cf. Lloyd, *loc. cit.* (Note 1) 87. See also Lloyd 78 for an anthology of negative appraisals of the *Timaeus*, some of them utterly naive in their disregard of elementary historical considerations. Lloyd himself while anxious to be fair and while free of some

will not balance the damage done by the prominence of soul in subjects where it has no place. The same critics would not even allow Plato's introduction of mathematics to be a pioneer's work, since in their opinion it does not create the type of science to which the future belonged but by its arbitrary and apriori decisions ominously resembles numerology and number-mysticism.

From this disturbing situation two principal questions arise: Did Plato's authority impede the progress of empirical science and the study of mechanical causalities? And, more important still, is it legitimate to regard his own system as scientific? I must limit myself to a minimum of suggestions. You have seen how, beginning with Aristotle and continuing in later biology, Plato's concept of purpose was increasingly purged of moral ingredients; it continued and still continues as "function." When the emphasis shifted to observation and material accumulated, many Platonic doctrines were abandoned, others modified. Aristotle's revision of Plato's physics often replaces one apriori theory by another; but in his biology empirical investigation takes over. It flourished in Aristotle's school and thence passed on to Alexandria, that great center of Hellenistic research. But for the scientists of Alexandria Plato's name was by no means anathema. The construction of the planetary movements as circles was welcomed and in principle accepted; where it proved too simple, it became "with centric and eccentric scribbled over, cycle and epicycle." [36] That Euclid produced his mathematical "Elements" in a spirit faithful to the Platonic traditions I have mentioned.[37] If one more illustration is desired,

---

prejudices, nevertheless tends to judge Plato by the standard of modern science. The soundness of this procedure is open to serious doubts. That an entirely new type of science arose in the 17th century is no longer a secret. Marie Boas, *The Establishment of the Mechanical Philosophy (Osiris 10, 1952, 412 ff.)*, H. Butterfield, *The Origins of Modern Science* (New York, 1951) and others have shown the fundamental difference between this modern science and the Platonic-Aristotelian science which is at the base of the mediaeval world picture. See the admirable conclusions drawn by E. M. Adams in his *Philosophy and the Modern Mind* (Chapel Hill, N.C., 1976), 48 ff. To "evaluate" Plato's science by criteria reflecting a totally different outlook can only breed confusion. (I hope that my own comparison, above, p. 97, with the habits of modern chemistry will not be misunderstood as a "vindication" or "evaluation".)

[36] Milton, *P.L.* VIII 83 f.

[37] Historians of mathematics do not find it easy to assess the relation between Euclid and the mathematical achievements of the Platonic Academy. K. von Fritz, *op. cit.* (n. 3) *pass.*, esp. pp. 361 ff., 375 f. marks a progress, not least by using the valuable information contained in Aristotle's *Ana-*

I should put forward the name of the illustrious geographer Eratos-thenes, nicknamed the "new Plato"; his startling accomplishment of calculating the circumference of the Earth—how accurately is not certain; at the worst 12%, at best less than 1% off—owes much to Platonic inspirations; for it used ratios or proportions, topics that had fascinated him in the *Timaeus*.[38] On the other hand, there were after the *Timaeus* no more brilliant cosmologies of the Presocratic type, no large systems relying on "material" or mechani-cal causation. But it would be rash to hold Plato responsible. The climate of thought in the Hellenistic centuries did not favor such ventures. In the one instance where such a system was revived and brought up-to-date ulterior reasons were at work. A universe which functioned mechanically freed man from all worry and fear of the gods and allowed him to find the source of happiness in his own mind. This is what Epicurus and what Hellenistic man desired.

Now as for our final question, whether Plato's system may be considered science, this is in part a matter of definition, and Plato himself would probably react to our answer, whether yes or no, with the utmost indifference. In the course of my Lecture I referred to the good number of centuries that would be in basic sympathy with the Platonic outlook, in contrast to a bare handful that are on the modern side. But I have no desire to settle the issue by a majority vote of centuries. Rather should I join the peerless Frances Yates and others in the protest against inter-preting "the science of the past solely from the forward-looking point of view, picking from the context... only what seems to point in the direction of modern developments." To which protest I should add the question how I might know about the "directions of modern developments." [39] Fifty years ago when I received a

---

*lytica Posteriora* I, which has far too often been ignored or minimized. Another important source, Proclus' *Prolegomena to Euclid* which contains historical material derived from Eudemus of Rhodes, a pupil of Aristotle, may receive more attention now that it has become available in the attrac-tive translation of Glenn R. Morrow (*Proclus. A Commentary to the First Book of Euclid*, Princeton, N.J., 1970).

[38] See my paper "Eratosthenes as Platonist and poet," *TAPA* 73, 1942, 192 ff. (= *Kleine Schriften* I 203 ff.). Problems regarding the accuracy of Eratosthenes' calculation are discussed by J. Oliver Thompson, *History of Anc. Geography* (Cambr., 1948) 161 f.

[39] See her paper "The Hermetic Tradition in the Renaissance" in Charles S. Singleton (ed.), *Art, Science and History in the Renaissance* (Baltimore, 1967) 270. Mary Hesse *Proc. Brit. Acad.* 58 (1972) 276 ff. esp. 285 ff. calls for a "dialogue" between past and present science; what she has in mind is

smattering of physics it moved in one direction; now outstanding physicists assure me that I need not regret having forgotten most or all of what I then acquired because it was misconceived and futile, the direction in which it moves today being quite different. In mathematics too there has been a reorientation. But a standard of truth ought to be stable, absolute, not bending or yielding to "relativity." Therefore I have deliberately refrained from collecting recent pronouncements by Heisenberg and others that came my way, indicating that physics is swinging back to Plato and the new emphasis is on structure and even—who would have believed it—on beauty. I also refrain from reminding you of the grandiose physical and philosophical cosmology of Whitehead, in whose *Process and Reality* scholars discovered so much of Plato that the next learned commentator of the *Timaeus* had to read even more of Whitehead into Plato.[40] Nature, it has been said, has answers ready for almost any questions; what questions are asked depends again largely on the outlook and the intellectual climate of a period—though Plato is an exception; in his case it depends on individual genius.[41] Surely, modern science has done better by the criterion of practical applicability, of use for the good of man. But this "good" is not the Platonic "good," and again where fifty years ago people found only "good for man," to-day they wonder whether the ill for man does not outweigh the good. The Greeks were on the whole too aristocratic to demand practical gain from science. Perhaps we had better drop the question what kind of science is the true science. If modern science has the advantage of producing some material good and comfort—and further advantages too of course—Plato's excels in other respects. It excels by orienting itself so resolutely by the "good" of the whole; by being eminently synthetic, completely free of compartments. It honors man without flattering him. Tentative in its propositions, it does not claim for scientific conclusions more certainty and validity than for moral principles. And finally it excels quite simply by its beauty.

---

something more sophisticated than much that has hitherto passed as "history."

[40] The reference is to A. E. Taylor, *A Commentary on Plato's Timaeus* (Oxford, 1928) and to Cornford's critical opinion about it (XI f.).

[41] Cf. C. S. Lewis, *op. cit.* (n. 11) 223; see his entire "Epilogue" (pp. 216 ff.).

# INDEX LOCORUM

Page-references are given in italics.

# GENERAL INDEX